Unbelievable Crimes Volume Eleven

Unbelievable Crimes, Volume 11

Daniela Airlie

Published by Daniela Airlie, 2024.

UNBELIEVABLE CRIMES VOLUME ELEVEN

First edition. June 7, 2024.

Written by Daniela Airlie.

Table of Contents

Introduction

Welcome to *Unbelievable Crimes Volume Eleven*. For those new to the series, let me briefly introduce the anthologies' premise: to cover lesser-known (or hastily forgotten) true crime stories.

In this volume, I cover 20 true tales of crime, murder, and mayhem. Amid this volume's morbid and macabre tales lie some truly wicked cases that stay with you long after you've learned about them.

Twisted teenagers, perverse individuals who are seen as trusted members of the community, and violent spouses make up some of the perpetrators in this volume. Many of the culprits in this installment were captured for the crimes they committed, though their wrongdoing is often so heinous, I wonder if there's such a thing as adequate justice when a life has been taken.

As always, let me remind you: this book details suffering and descriptions of real crimes—bear this in mind if you feel this topic is too heavy for you. With that said, let's begin.

A Date With Evil

Dating apps have become a part of modern life. When you ask a couple how they met nowadays, you'll be just as likely to be told "online dating" as much as you're likely to hear that they met in a bar or at work. Like many things in the technological age, this aspect of modern life doesn't come without its dangers and pitfalls.

With online dating, you're somewhat forced to take people at their word—that they are who they say they are. If you get chatting with someone and begin to feel comfortable enough to meet in real life, you forgo a step often taken for granted in years gone by: the ability to get to know that person in person before agreeing to go on a date. Feeling things out via your smartphone just isn't the same as doing it in person. Certainly, the nefarious among us can hide many of their red flag traits behind a phone screen.

The haunting story of Grace Millane could have you rethinking your approach to modern dating.

Grace had not long graduated college when she decided to pursue her dream of traveling. The 21-year-old took a gap year to explore parts of the world she'd only dreamed of visiting while growing up in the U.K. One of those places was New Zealand, where she'd wind up meeting 26-year-old Jesse Kempson, who she met on a dating app.

On the eve of her 22nd birthday—the day she met up with Kempson—he would kill her. In an all-too-common theme in cases like this, Kempson had a known history of violence against women.

Grace Millane grew up in Essex, U.K., along with her two brothers. David and Gillian Millane doted on their three children, and the Millane siblings would grow up to be outgoing and fun-loving young adults. Grace ended up graduating from the University of Lincoln with a marketing degree, and after weighing up the pros and cons of taking a gap year to travel, she chose to make the leap and spend time abroad before embarking on a career.

In October 2018, she made a social media post bidding farewell to the U.K. and was waved off by her family as she made her way to South America. For six weeks, she backpacked and explored the picturesque landscapes, making temporary friends and taking in the culture as she went. She loved every minute of it.

Grace then headed to New Zealand, where she again met fellow backpackers and made short-term companionships as part of her adventure. However, as exciting as it was to meet fleeting friends, Grace craved a little more depth and human connection. She'd been using a dating app while she was traveling, which helped her meet fellow solo backpackers. On December 1, 2018, she would match with Jesse Kempson.

The pair exchanged pleasantries and began chatting. Grace would tell Kempson that it was her birthday the following day, but she had no plans to celebrate. After chatting more, they eventually added each other on social media and made plans to meet that evening.

Their meeting was captured on CCTV, where Kempson embraced Grace before they headed for drinks together. Analyzing the footage, there was no awkward hug or hesitancy from either party. Both Grace and Kempson appeared comfortable and happy to see one another.

Kempson, who was familiar with the area, showed Grace the various bars Auckland had to offer. He introduced her to various new drinks and advised her on the best cocktails to order. They flitted from a burger bar to a Mexican cafe to a spot that sold traditional sangria. Again, this was all captured on CCTV.

To the naked eye, they looked like a young couple getting to know one another. Grace leans in intently as Kempson chats away, perhaps filling her full of lies, much like he did his other conquests.

Unbeknown to Grace, Kempson was a serial dating app user. In the weeks leading up to their meet, he'd been incredibly busy swiping and liking young women on his dating app of choice. He would meet up with one date and tell her he was related to a celebrity. He would tell others he was a successful businessman scouring Auckland for possible bar and restaurant locations to set up shop. In reality, he was a barman and sometimes worked as a laborer. It's unclear why he felt the need to lie about his career and familial ties.

As well as the pointless lies, some of Kempson's dates were also subjected to horrific sexual experiences with him. He would tell them he enjoys "rough" encounters and ended up strangling one date so violently she feared for her life.

As is the nature of dating apps, Grace had no clue about Kempson's history. By this point though, he had been exposed as abusive and deceptive by more than a handful of women, some of whom he'd cohabited with.

At one point, Kempson had replied to a house share advert placed by a houseful of women. The ad made it clear the household was made up of women only. Still, the housemates decided to take a chance on the male applicant since his credentials were impressive. Upon meeting Kempson, the women felt he was charming and respectable. He was invited to join the house share.

It wouldn't take long for his veneer to drop, though. Pretty soon, the women who lived in the property would make sure they weren't left alone with Kempson, and one was made to feel so uncomfortable around him that she slept with a knife beside her bed. He went from unassuming to creepy quickly, particularly when he'd consumed alcohol.

If you judged it by the two hours' worth of CCTV footage available of the pair, Grace's date with Kempson looked to be going great. The couple shared kisses, intense conversation, and ample cocktails.

At 9:41 pm, CCTV caught the pair at CityLife hotel, where Kempson was living. Kempson fumbles around in his wallet for his room key before the couple head out of the elevator. This footage would depict some of Grace's final moments. Before the night ends, she'd be dead.

Only Grace and Kempson know what went on behind the closed door of room 308. However, one of them would never get the chance to tell their story, and the other one is a serial liar.

As December 2 rolled around, Grace's friends and family all texted her birthday wishes. She didn't reply. She didn't acknowledge any birthday messages on social media, either. She didn't return any calls. Her family began to worry since Grace had been in constant contact with them since she left the U.K. She'd frequently sent pictures of her adventures and updates on her whereabouts to her parents, who grew increasingly concerned as the days passed without any word from Grace.

On December 5, they contacted the police. The family was hopeful that nothing sinister had happened to Grace; perhaps her phone had broken or been stolen while she was out celebrating her birthday. However, parental gut instinct saw David and Gillian fear the worst. Auckland police began their search for Grace, which began at the hostel she'd been staying at. A quick review of the hostel's records and CCTV proved she'd not been back since she left on the evening of December 1.

The police then trawled Grace's social media for clues. One comment in particular piqued their interest: it was a comment left on the night of her disappearance by a man named "Jesse Shane." Unlike other friends and commenters on Grace's page, this man was local, and it seemed the pair had just connected on social media the day she disappeared.

The police contacted him and requested he come to the station for questioning. Jesse did as they asked, and when he arrived at the station, he was dressed in a three-piece suit. The investigator who questioned Jesse Shane—aka Kempson—found his attire "odd" but conceded that there was no law against being odd. Jesse wasn't explicitly told why he was at the station but was asked about his whereabouts on the night of December 1.

He told them he met up with Grace, told them where they went that night, and described kissing her goodbye before taking himself to a local bar to drink alone. Unbeknown to Kempson, the police were busy piecing CCTV footage together in the background, and it became clear he was lying. Well, he told the truth about the bars he and Grace went to but blatantly lied when it came to the "going for drinks alone" part.

The footage clearly showed him taking Grace back to his hotel room. The cameras would never capture Grace leaving the hotel. His lies—which the police didn't call him out on straight away, instead letting him weave his web of untruths—turned him from a witness to a prime suspect.

Authorities were also tracing Kempson's whereabouts in the aftermath of Grace's disappearance. The day after he met up with Grace, he ended up going on a date with another woman he met on a dating app. Once he bid her farewell, he took himself shopping to make some suspicious purchases: bleach, a suitcase, and a rented carpet cleaning machine.

The police quickly obtained a warrant to search Kempson's room and analyze his cell phone. His search history was chilling.

In the early hours of December 2, he'd made internet searches for pornography as well as "hottest fire," "large bags," and "flesh-eating birds." He also searched for the Waitakere ranges, which offer 16000 hectares of rainforest. It would seem Kempson wasn't searching because he wanted to explore the range, but rather, he was looking for a place to dispose of Grace's body.

If this evidence wasn't incriminating enough, the images found on his device were sickeningly damning. Pictures of Grace lying dead were found on Kempson's camera roll. He'd maneuvered her body into different poses for his own twisted pleasure.

The net had well and truly fallen down onto Kempson, who knew the evidence against him was stacking up rapidly.

Meanwhile, the forensic team was searching his hotel room. They used luminol to trace any blood that may have been cleaned up inside his accommodation. Luminol can pick up blood that's been thoroughly scrubbed clean, and it turns neon blue when the chemical touches it. Kempson's hotel room was turned into one big blue glow with the amount of blood the luminol picked up.

There was no way this could have been explained away as a nosebleed or accidental bump to the head; the amount of blood was life-ending. Grace's body was found on the afternoon of December 9, over a week after her death.

With all of this wildly incriminating evidence piling up, the police confronted Kempson with it. He suddenly changed his story; he admitted that Grace had died in his hotel room, but it was accidental. They'd had "rough sex," and part way through, he discovered Grace was no longer breathing. In a panic, he says he bundled her into a suitcase and buried her in Waitakere ranges.

Still, his tale didn't add up. He didn't try to call the police when he discovered Grace wasn't breathing. Despite Kempson saying he dialed 911 but didn't hit the call button out of fear of prison, it seems he had no intention of ringing the authorities. Not only that, in the hours after Grace's murder, he'd watched pornography. Thereafter, he'd taken pictures of Grace's corpse. He'd engaged in hours of debauchery with a dead body in his hotel room. There was no sign of panic or dismay at what he'd done. Quite the opposite in fact.

His lack of remorse was further seen when he went on a date that same day as Grace lay dead in his hotel room.

Chillingly, the woman he went on a date with would tell the police of an eerie anecdote he told her: how one of his friends had accidentally killed his partner during rough sex. His "friend" went to jail for this "mistake," causing Kempson to mull over the idea of one mishap ruining a man's life forever. What the woman believed to be a macabre tale was, in fact, Kempson's reality. However, there was no "mistake"—it was a cold-blooded murder.

Needless to say, when Kempson asked the woman for a second date, she politely declined.

Still, Kempson wouldn't admit culpability. The trial began on November 4, 2019, though throughout this, he still insisted the death was accidental and stressed that Grace had asked to be strangled. His defense against the murder charge was a taboo one: rough sex leading to accidental death.

The defense is akin to a rapist claiming their interaction with the victim was consensual. It puts the defense into "he said, she said" territory that can be incredibly hard to prove either way. In this case, however, there was enough evidence to show that Kempson's murder of Grace was far from accidental. Sadly, in many cases over the years, this defense has proven successful, where killers have either been allowed to remain free or have been given the lesser sentence of manslaughter for their crimes.

To further combat his claim that Kempson didn't mean to kill Grace, the prosecution brought in Dr. Simon Stables, who would testify that in order to kill the victim, the accused would have had to apply forceful pressure to her neck for at least five minutes.

Five minutes may not seem like a long time. However, consider someone asking you to make a five-minute speech that requires you to use every last second of that time frame; it would drag on for what felt like an hour. For Grace, those five minutes would have felt like forever. Seconds feeling like minutes. For Kempson, to keep such a tight grip on Grace's neck for over five minutes would have taken some strength.

The trial of Grace's murder saw Kempson's name in the press, though he did fight successfully to keep it repressed for a short while. Despite this, many of his victims came forward, telling of his violent sexual crimes toward them. Almost all of these women had met Kempson on dating apps.

One woman accused Kempson of violently raping her. She said during the assault, his eyes were "popping" out of his head, and his face was full of anger. These images, as you can imagine, continued to haunt her. She didn't feel able to go to the police after the attack, but once she saw his name in the paper after Grace Millane's murder, she came forward. So did a number of other women. Some of them he'd directly abused, others he'd confessed his desire for strangulation and dominance during sex.

A former girlfriend came forward to accuse Kempson of sexually assaulting her at knifepoint. It seems the serial sex offender had been getting away with his sick crimes for years, and he felt untouchable. So much so that he felt able to escalate to murder.

The trial took place over three weeks, after which Kempson was found guilty of Grace's murder. He was handed life in jail with a minimum of 17 years to be served. Naturally, Kempson appealed. This was rejected, though he would again appeal his sentence, still claiming that Grace's death was accidental. By 2021, he'd exhausted all of his appeal options, costing the taxpayers of New Zealand over $400,000 in the process.

Sadly, Grace's father, David, died of cancer in 2020. Though he suffered immensely in the years leading up to his death, there is one small mercy for the bereft father: he was able to see his daughter's killer put behind bars, possibly for life.

In the aftermath of her daughter's murder, Gillian Millane founded the charity "Love Grace" to help women affected by domestic violence. The charity gives those affected handbags filled with essentials such as toiletries and hygiene products. By the end of 2023, they'd donated over 15,000 handbags throughout the U.K. as well as overseas.

The Megalomaniac

Picture this terrifying scenario: you're hundreds of feet below sea level, trapped inside a small submarine with a sadistic killer. He wants nothing more than to see you full of fear and terror, begging for your life. There is no way out from the tiny metal vessel you're in. The killer is intent on not only ending your life but making you suffer unimaginable cruelty before your death.

It sounds like a horror movie. But this scenario was very real for journalist Kim Wall, who found herself trapped underwater with serial entrepreneur—and sadist—Peter Madsen.

Madsen forced his victim to endure sickening bouts of torture while he kept her hostage in his submarine. The vessel, which he'd built after a successful crowdfunding, was his pride and joy. The inception of the sub, named UC3 Nautilus, garnered a lot of attention from the press, leading to the inventor receiving a lot of media attention, too.

One journalist who was captivated by the submarine's construction was Kim Wall. She sought out an interview with Peter Madsen to learn more about his self-taught engineering skills.

Little did Kim know that Madsen was incredibly dangerous as well as exceptionally intelligent. In fact, he even referred to himself as "sadistic" to his friends. Madsen's peers knew he had a darker side, but this was often seen as part of his quirky persona. If only people knew just how dark and depraved he truly was behind the thin, eccentric varnish.

But how could someone with so much promise and potential harbor such sadistic desires? As true crime followers often come to realize, when we consume stories like this, a person's veneer is no indicator as to how good (or bad) a person they are.

Some of the most kind-hearted people on the planet have the moodiest dispositions. Some of the more cruel, heartless people appear jovial and generous. This notion is most certainly verified when you explore true crime cases; we must never judge a book by its cover.

Born in Denmark in 1971, Madsen had a relatively normal childhood, though his father was over three decades older than his mother. The patriarch, Carl Madsen, was allegedly abusive towards his wife's children from other marriages. He would beat his unwanted stepchildren, which saw the terrified mother flee the marital home with her four sons in tow. There were never any accusations of Carl beating his biological son, and as Madsen grew older, he would eventually seek out his father and form a relationship with him.

The father and son shared an interest in engineering, specifically the building of rockets. With his father's encouragement and help from his physics teacher, 15-year-old Madsen built his own rocket and launched it in the spring of 1986. He'd spent countless hours crafting the rocket in his father's workshop, and upon liftoff, it reached over 300 feet in the air before hurtling to the ground.

It was an impressive feat for a young boy and certainly impressed his father. However, by this point, Madsen was still in his teens, and his father was elderly. Poor health began to take over. In 1990, when Madsen was just 18, his father passed away.

Still, the young man's love of engineering and building things didn't quell after his father's death. In fact, it only grew, and Madsen began connecting with established engineers and joining the local rocket club, seeking the mentor he'd lost in his father. He dropped out of education after high school, which isn't the norm for someone who wanted to pursue a career in engineering, but Madsen was confident in his abilities.

Despite his lack of qualifications, he managed to convince various local businesses and organizations to fund his varying inventions. It wouldn't take long, however, for those tasked with working alongside Madsen to be privy to his more sinister side. While at first, he seemed enthusiastic and eager to be part of a team when tackling his projects, he soon became power-hungry and controlling.

It wasn't just his in-work behavior that raised eyebrows; his extracurricular activities were widely discussed by his peers, too. Madsen was known to throw wild parties, perhaps better described as "orgies," and was a self-described "sadist." He used the word specifically to describe himself to his co-workers, a comment they likely brushed off as nothing more than a little odd from the highly odd man. Madsen was truly eccentric, after all.

In reality, he was showing them who he really was. And, when someone shows you who they are, you best believe it to be true.

Madsen had made a name for himself in the mid-2000s, and by 2008, he was well known as an unconventional inventor in his home country of Denmark, achieving a small celebrity status. By this point, he'd just launched his third self-designed submarine, UC3 Nautilus. The vessel was constructed by a team of volunteers who believed in Madsen's vision of the submarine.

It seemed that the inventor, no matter how difficult or insufferable he could become, always managed to get others excited about his visions. This appears to have played a big part in his success.

When the UC3 was lowered into the water in May 2008, crowds of people gathered to watch, as did the press. It was an intriguing story; a self-taught engineer had successfully crowdfunded a number of innovative creations that he then brought to life, culminating in this impressive submarine. The story was especially intriguing for Kim Wall, who had followed Madsen and his designs for years.

While Madsen was creating his inventions in the 90s, Kim was merely dreaming of being a big-time journalist at school. In 2009, Madsen was the focus of a documentary that followed him and his creation of the submarines, and the young aspiring magazine journalist watched in amazement.

By the mid-2010s, Kim was pursuing her dream career as a young 20-something. Around the same time, Madsen was still giving interviews and press releases to various news establishments, basking in his newfound fame. Perhaps Kim would get that interview with the inventor after all; interest in his creations showed no sign of waning.

Madsen didn't want to stop at just submarines; he wanted to create rockets and send them to space. He eventually connected with spaceflight architect Kristian von Bengtson, and the pair were due to work on a project together. Until the relationship soured, and the duo went their separate ways, which saw Madsen create his own solo project, named the "Rocket Madsen Space Lab." After the falling out, in a show of what may be seen as pettiness, Madsen set up the workshop for the lab directly across the road from his old workshop with Kristian.

By this point, Madsen was extremely wealthy. He was an admired inventor, entrepreneur, and a promising member of the spaceflight community. With his newly acquired wealth came the apparent freedom for Madsen to expose the darker aspects of his personality even further. Often, people who accumulate a lot of money in a short space of time tend also to gain the notion that they can buy themselves a ticket to be lawless.

For Madsen, he would host wild parties that were allegedly not only attended by people but "human robots" that he'd built. These parties would see attendees stripped naked, mingling with the robots and other guests as the DJ played loud music, like a scene from a late 80s sci-fi movie. While throwing these bizarre yet lavish events, Madsen would confess to his peers that he was a keen swinger who was also—there's that word again—a sadist.

Yet again, people believed Madsen was simply a quirky inventor who was a little too open about his unsavory preferences.

In 2011, Madsen got married, though he would insist to his coworkers and friends that he was still free to see other people. It's unclear if his wife knew of this arrangement, but getting married didn't quell Madsen's habit of attending sex parties and engaging in orgies.

By 2017, journalist Kim Wall, who'd been following Madsen's rise to prominence for years, contacted him for an interview. His rags-to-riches story of a self-taught engineer becoming a revered inventor captivated her. Madsen, by now in his mid-40s, agreed to the interview.

Unbeknownst to Kim, she was arranging her date with death. Not just death; brutal sadism.

On August 10, 2017, the pair were exchanging texts in the lead-up to their meet later that day. The journalist was due to take a trip with Madsen in his sub as she interviewed him about his life, successes, and plans. "The ship is ready and in good shape. Just waiting for the reporter," Madsen would text that afternoon.

When Kim met Madsen at the dock, he came bearing coffee and cookies. A friendly gesture that perhaps masqueraded his true intentions: to gain Kim's trust and emit a "nice guy," image. After chatting for a bit and breaking the ice, Madsen would suggest taking a ride in UC3 Nautilus. Having an hour or so aboard the submarine was important for Kim so she could flesh out her article and make it as in-depth as possible. After all, she'd been pursuing this interview for a while and knew she could create an excellent write-up about Madsen and his inventions.

Just before getting in the submarine, Kim texted her boyfriend. Ominously, it read: "I'm still alive." While it was a joke, the bantersome text is sinister in hindsight. She followed up with, "But I'm going down now. I love you."

It would be the last Ole Stobbe would hear from his girlfriend.

Hours passed, and Ole began to panic when Kim didn't text again. The clock hit 10 pm, then 11 pm, then 12 am without any contact from Kim. She was still unable to take calls, suggesting she was still in the submarine. Surely not, though; something sinister must have happened. Kim wouldn't simply ghost her partner. Her last text to him expressed her love for him. Ole knew something bad had happened, though even his wildest nightmares couldn't have imagined just how bad.

In the early hours of the following morning, Ole called the police to report her missing.

He told them everything he knew: where she'd gone, who she was with, and what time he'd expected her home. The submarine experience was only supposed to last two hours, tops. A search for the young journalist ensued.

Later that morning, Madsen was found sinking in his submarine. A technical fault had seemingly caused him to become trapped inside as the submarine plunged further into the sea near Koge Bay. Luckily, he was near a lighthouse when his submersible was spotted, and he was quickly rescued.

First responders were shocked to discover Madsen was alone on UC3 Nautilus. When asked where Kim Wall was, Madsen insisted he'd dropped her at the harbor the evening prior. As far as he was concerned, he'd left her safely on land before he climbed back on UC3. It was at this point he ran into trouble, and the vessel began to sink. At least, that's what Madsen told authorities.

His story was, at best, suspicious. Perhaps Madsen knew he wasn't truly fooling the police with his insistence that he'd left Kim safe and sound on land. Plus, the "sinking" of his submarine seemed all too convenient. It would only take a day for Madsen to change his story.

In his new version of events, Madsen said Kim had fatally banged her head while aboard the UC3. As a result, he cast her body to sea. His explanations just didn't make sense. Despite being seen as an intelligent man, Madsen was far from it during his interactions with the police. As his stories changed, his credibility whittled down to zero.

Almost two weeks after Kim had disappeared, a cyclist happened upon a macabre discovery as they rode along a beach. It was a human torso. Not just a torso, a horribly mutilated torso filled with stab marks covering it. Sickeningly, a great deal of those stab wounds were on the victim's genitals.

The body was identified as Kim Wall.

The forensic team found no traces of blunt force trauma to Kim's head, rebutting Madsen's version of events that she'd hit her head. When presented with the gruesome new evidence, Madsen changed his story again. This time, he said Kim had died from carbon monoxide poisoning. To get her off the vessel, he chopped her up and cast her out to sea with metal attached to her in a bid to ensure she sank to the sea floor.

Madsen claimed that the only way to dispose of Kim's body was to dismember her. He had no explanation for the abundance of stab marks found on her. By no means could he explain these away as accidental, like he claimed her death was.

The suspect was detained while the police collated their evidence. Investigators would obtain a warrant for Madsen's cell phone, which revealed a sick search history. In the hours leading up to Kim's death, he'd looked up girls being beheaded and searched for videos that depicted "agony."

A further search of his computer found a collection of snuff films. Madsen had some truly sick material on his hard drive, particularly of women being brutally tortured before their deaths. One of them saw the victim's life ended by knives and spears. When Madsen was confronted with these videos—which lined up with what Kim was subjected to prior to her death—he said it was purely coincidental.

A few months later, other parts of Kim's body were found near where her torso was recovered. The jig was up for Madsen. Though, he still refused to admit what he'd done. He'd changed his story multiple times: first, he said he'd dropped Kim off at the dock. Then, he said she'd banged her head and died. His final story was that she'd died of carbon monoxide poisoning.

When asked why he kept changing his story, Madsen claimed he lied initially to spare Kim's family from the details surrounding her death. *Not to spare himself from justice but to spare them from the tragic truth.*

In mid-January 2018, Madsen was formally charged with Kim's murder. In addition, due to the horrific mutilation of her corpse, Madsen was charged with indecent handling of a corpse and the sexual assault of Kim Wall. The trial began that spring.

Still, Madsen wouldn't confess what really happened on the UC3. The prosecution put it to the jury that Madsen cruelly tortured Kim before either strangling her to death or slitting her throat. A definite cause of death couldn't be ascertained from the body, but Madsen had been watching and searching for videos that involved those twisted murder methods prior to meeting with Kim.

It was also ascertained that Madsen had deliberately sunk the UC3 to cover his tracks. He did so in front of a lighthouse, a place that would ensure his discovery and rescue.

On April 25, 2018, he was convicted of Kim's murder and handed life behind bars. Naturally, he appealed his sentence, though his appeal was rejected.

Madsen was only in prison for four months when he was attacked by another inmate, causing the disgraced inventor to be hospitalized. In 2020, he finally admitted to killing Kim Wall, though his confession was more matter-of-fact than fuelled by remorse or guilt.

His lack of remorse was further seen when, in late 2020, he managed to escape from prison. Not only did Madsen admit his guilt (though he didn't divulge exactly how he killed Kim or any further details), he felt he shouldn't serve his punishment for the crime. Which, some may argue, doesn't come close to matching the crime.

While serving his sentence at Herstedvester Prison in Denmark, Madsen created a fake bomb belt and makeshift gun to threaten a prison employee into letting him walk free. It seems even life behind bars didn't quell his desire to invent, though it now appeared his inventions were weapons. Madsen then managed to make it over the prison walls and raced as fast as he could to freedom.

He tasted all but five minutes of freedom before the guards caught up with him. Before hauling him back to his cell, there was a few hours' standoff between Madsen and the authorities—they weren't sure if his bomb belt was real, so they were extra cautious when apprehending him.

Still, once they had him in cuffs, it was only a five-minute walk back to Herstedvester. When asked what he was planning to do upon his escape, Madsen said he would carjack his way to Germany.

His bid for freedom—and the violent way in which he planned to maintain his freedom—will serve to affect any future parole hearings he may have adversely.

Violent Voyeur

Margaret Douglas was an impressive 98 years old. She had no plans on stopping there, though; she was adamant she would make it to 100. It was her dream to be a centenarian, of which there are only around half a million around the world. She was just two short years off her goal when her life was cruelly ended, all for a killer's twisted kicks.

Margaret lived in the small city of Wadsworth, Ohio, surrounded by her family and a small handful of friends who aided the woman in her day-to-day business. While she was physically still quite capable, there was no denying that almost ten decades of living and raising her family had taken its toll on Margaret. She would need help with certain household tasks, but aside from that, the grandmother was admirably self-sufficient.

The animal-lover enjoyed pruning her garden and watching baseball. Margaret would be on her sofa watching the TV when she wasn't in her flower garden. On April 6, 2018, she was resting up on the sofa as some random program played in the background as she dozed. Margaret wound up falling into a deep sleep. So deep that she didn't hear an intruder making their way into her home.

Three days later, the Wadsworth Police Department received a call from Margarets' family. They'd not heard from her in a few days, which was unusual. The woman always ensured she kept in touch and rarely skipped a day without talking to her family.

When they couldn't reach her, panic set in. Officers went to Margaret's home to check in on her, though she was nowhere to be seen.

It was almost unheard of for Margaret to go far from home, let alone stay out for extended periods of time. The family knew something was amiss, and on April 9, Margaret's nephew escorted officers to carry out a more thorough search of her property.

Howard Leasure was close to his aunt, and his gut feeling told him that if they found some clues, they wouldn't lead them to anything but bad news.

Howard scoured the property, looking for anything out of place or something to help guide them in figuring out what had happened to Margaret. He combed the living room and the kitchen and made his way into his aunt's bedroom. Nothing seemed untoward. He opened up the wardrobe and noticed some shoes strewn on the floor. *Not like Aunt Margaret to simply throw her things in the wardrobe carelessly.* Beside the shoes was a pile of clothing, again just carelessly tossed, not folded as Margaret usually would do.

He kneeled closer and moved the items, only to discover his beloved aunt's body underneath the pile of clothes. The shoes he'd just noticed were still on Margaret's feet. Howard stumbled back and collapsed into tears.

The officers at the home quickly made their way to the crime scene. It was clear this was no accidental death; Margret's clothing was torn, and she showed blatant bruising on her neck. She also had injuries to her face. Her body had begun decomposing, meaning she'd been dead for days.

Investigators swarmed Margaret's home as she was taken for forensic examination. Her home was searched, and her purse was notably missing. This led the investigators to go down the road of thinking this was a burglary gone wrong. Then, they found a plastic glove outside Margaret's home, suggesting whoever broke in had planned the invasion.

The community was small and tight-knit, with the neighborhood making sure to take care of Margaret when she needed it. The woman had no enemies, nor had she fallen out with any of her neighbors. It just wasn't in Margaret's nature to have disputes with people, much less had she ever done anything to upset anyone.

Margaret's family were interviewed to see if investigators could get even a sliver of a clue as to who may have carried out this macabre act. The interviews led officers to one of Margaret's friends named David.

David was close to Margaret and would often come around to her house and do any chores or tasks she was unable to carry out. Officers reached out and tried to contact him to no avail. It felt like he was avoiding the police, though they soon caught up with him when they found him loitering outside Margaret's home. Naturally, this piqued their suspicion. Why was he hanging around the crime scene?

Investigators finally managed to question David. The man didn't help quell investigators' suspicion of him when he was able to tell them details of the murder and that he was an old neighbor of Margaret's who wanted to know how the investigation was coming along. The more officers looked into David, the more he seemed intrigued by the case, too intrigued. He was reported to have told other members of the neighborhood that he was worried his fingerprints were in Margaret's home, thus implicating him.

Naturally, this caused investigators to haul David in for formal questioning. He told them about the last time he saw Margaret, and retraced his steps the last time he visited her home. It was a few days prior to her body being found, and David told officers he couldn't find Margaret.

The way David talked saw the police escalate him from a person of interest to a possible suspect. They mentioned they'd found a glove outside Margaret's home and told David they'd like a DNA sample from him to cross-reference against the DNA found in the glove. To the investigators' surprise, he was more than happy to offer a sample.

When testing showed that David hadn't used the glove, the police began to lower their suspicions of him. They also checked out his alibis for his whereabouts around the time Margaret was killed, and they proved he was telling the truth.

He wasn't in the area. It seems David's extreme intrigue toward the murder was just that: he'd simply wanted to find out who'd killed his dear friend Margaret.

With David now out of the suspect line, leads were drying up for investigators. They were clinging to hope that the autopsy would return some solid evidence. In a strange twist, when the report came back, it noted that Margaret hadn't been raped, despite her underwear being ripped and torn. It was clear there was an element of sexual gratification in the killing, but it was unusual for the findings to reveal no traces of this.

So, without anywhere else to turn to, officers began trawling through the petty criminals in the area. They now suspected that whoever killed Margaret had escalated from burglaries and other violent crimes to cold-blooded murder. After looking at the list of less serious crimes in the area, they found a break-in had occurred on a local construction site, where the criminal had accidentally dropped their phone during the burglary.

The phone led them directly to a teenager named Zach. Upon speaking with Zach, investigators weren't convinced they had a killer in their custody. He was meek, nervous, and keen to offer up answers to any questions they had. Unlike hardened criminals or remorseless lawbreakers, Zach wanted to comply.

He admitted he broke into the construction site but said he didn't do it alone and that it wasn't his idea. His friend, Gavon, coaxed him into it. In fact, Gavon had done things like this multiple times before and was a seasoned petty criminal. Zach seemed remorseful, so officers took his lead—however fruitless it may have been—and brought Gavon Ramsay in for questioning.

Gavon was only 17, so his mother came with him. Remarkably, as soon as he sat down in the interview room, he began spilling confession after confession: he admitted thieving cars and breaking into places to steal items. However, Gavon froze up after a while. He had something he wanted to tell the police about but couldn't do it in front of his mother. She would have to leave if he wasn't going to talk about it.

Once she left the room, the teenager shocked the police with his confession, though it wasn't the one they were looking for.

He admitted to meeting an older man on a dating website. When they met up, Gavon says he car-jacked the man's vehicle. He seemed upset over his admission. Investigators then decided this was the time to ask him about Margaret Douglas' murder, to which he quickly denied any involvement.

The boy's denial didn't convince the police.

So, they obtained a warrant to look through Gavon's phone. Their gut instinct was right. Through his camera roll were numerous pictures of Margaret laying asleep on her sofa moments before her life was ended. There was a video of her sleeping soundly as the voyeuristic teen leered over her.

Evidence in hand, officers formally arrested Gavon and confronted with the damning proof of his involvement in Margaret's murder. A confession quickly spilled.

Gavon said he got an adrenaline rush from entering properties illegally, as he had done the night of April 6 when he targeted Margaret's home. He spotted Margaret sleeping on the sofa and began recording her as she lay in a peaceful slumber. He did so for several minutes until she began to stir. According to Gavon, he panicked and dragged her from her comfortable spot on the sofa straight onto the floor and brutally strangled her to death. He claimed he had no idea what he was doing until it was over.

But there was more. Gavon knew it, and investigators knew it too. They'd seen the sickening footage on his phone. Gavon refused to talk about it, but investigators put the evidence to him anyway: video recordings of Gavon using Margaret's body for his own gratification. For two hours, he abused Margaret's corpse, videoing it as he carried out the attack.

The videos of him abusing Margaret were saved in a folder he labeled "dark." The folder was password-protected with the word "murder." It was clear there was zero remorse from the boy in the aftermath of the murder. Gavon refused to talk about it, but the police had the evidence clear as day on his cell phone.

After the prolonged abuse of the corpse, Gavon snuck away from the property. But not before shoving his victim into her tiny wardrobe and covering her with a pile of clothes.

A search warrant for the teenager's room was granted, and it made the case against him all the more damning if that were possible. Margaret's purse was found, as well as the glove that matched one found outside of her home. The prosecution team was grateful for Gavon's sloppiness; had he been more sophisticated, they may not have been able to build such a strong case against him.

Equally as terrifying was Gavon's personal journal. Inside, he wrote about his killer urges, detailing his desire to sexually assault his victims. There was no denying the 17-year-old basked in the idea of rape and murder, and it had simply been a matter of time before he carried out these depraved acts. It's not like his journal was hard to obtain either, or like he'd written the entry in code. All it would have taken was for someone—a concerned adult or friend—to open his journal at any page they chose, and they'd have been privy to the sadism that consumed Gavon's thoughts.

Gavon's mother was well aware of some of his issues. In fact, she'd taken him to counseling for what she believed to be depression. As a result, the teenager was placed on antidepressants. Later on, the mother would blame the prescription medication for changing her son for the worse, suggesting the tablets had been, in part, to blame for his killer urges.

A closer look into Gavon's life leading up to killing Margaret showed some dark and depraved tendencies. His phone history revealed a lot, as did his aspiration to work at a funeral home. In the year before the crime, applied for work at the local funeral chapel, which, in hindsight, is eerie. Knowing what we know now about Gavon's desire to desecrate the dead, it's a small mercy in this case that his application was declined.

In the aftermath of Margaret's brutal murder and the sick abuse after her death, Gavon admitted he felt no remorse. "I just continued to break into cars and smoke dope," he said of his feelings afterward. Worse still, he admitted that if he had gotten away with the murder, he would have continued to kill.

In January 2019, Gavon stood trial. It was put to the jury that the teenager planned the attack, having known Margaret from living around the same area as her. They suggested he didn't take weapons with him because he fully intended to kill the woman with his bare hands.

The stack of evidence against him ensured he was found guilty of Margaret's murder and was handed life in jail without the possibility of parole.

Some have suggested the sentence is harsh, considering Gavon was only in 11th grade when he carried out the crime. Other people believe rehabilitation is possible. However, criminals like Gavon—remorseless necrophiles—prove hard to reform. Think of fellow killers who desecrated the dead: Jeffery Dahmer, Ted Bundy, Jerry Brudos, or Ed Kemper. Each of these would have killed again, given a glimmer of a chance.

What are your thoughts on the sentencing? Too harsh or adequate? When I pondered this question, I did find myself wondering what would have happened if Dahmer, Bundy, or Brudos had been captured at age 17. My conclusion was that a whole list of victims would have been spared.

Could they have been rehabilitated? This is a much tougher question to answer. For Bundy, I think absolutely not. I think the same for Brudos. Dahmer claimed to have found religion and expressed regret for his spate of murders, but do I think he would have been able to stop himself from killing again if he had been released? I don't.

Then again, like with everything in life, there are exceptions to the rule. Could Gavon Ramsey be that exception? I'm not sure we'll ever find out.

Margaret Douglas' family remembers her as a "beautiful soul" who was an integral part of the family. They have one tiny solace from the whole ordeal: that her death meant Gavon Ramsay was locked away from any potential victims he had lined up.

A Gross Betrayal Of Trust

Abner Louima was born in 1966 in Haiti. In his early 20s, he immigrated to the USA, met the woman he would marry, and the pair would go on to have a child together. He would find work as a security guard so he could make sure his young family was taken care of.

However, what began as a picture-perfect story quickly turned sour in 1997 when Abner, at the hands of some brutish NYPD officers, was subjected to a sickening and sustained attack. He was beaten so badly by the officers that his teeth were broken. He suffered a punctured bladder, torn sphincter, and severed colon as a result of the most sickening part of the attack: he was raped by those who were entrusted to ensure the safety of the New York citizens.

As 1997 rolled around, Abner had taken to the role of family man well. He adored his wife and doted on his daughter, but finding steady work in his trained field was hard. A qualified electrical engineer, Abner struggled to get his foot in the door of any company that would offer this kind of role. So, he took on work as a security guard at a sewage plant in Brooklyn while he looked for engineering jobs.

On August 9 of that year, Abner was out with a couple of his friends at a nightclub in Brooklyn. As the last call for orders was announced at the bar, the patrons all rushed to get their final drinks of the night. Two women found themselves in an altercation with one another, and the nightclub-goers all crowded around to watch the fight that ensued.

Abner tried his best to intervene and separate the brawling women, but the rowdy crowd only got worse, and a melee broke out at the nightclub. The NYPD was called, and they dispatched several men to quell the disturbance: officers Justin Volpe, Charles Schwarz, Thomas Bruder, and Thomas Wiese.

After arriving at the scene, Volpe allegedly got aggressive with a member of the crowd, witnessed by Abner. The security guard confronted Volpe and began yelling at the heavy-handed officer. As the two men argued back and forth, another member of the crowd struck Officer Volpe. The man believed it was Abner who hit him and quickly got his fellow NYPD officers to apprehend the alleged attacker.

The cops set about beating Abner before cuffing him and taking him to the 70th Precinct. On the way to the station, the officers continued their beating of Abner, hitting him with their radios and batons.

The violence was only just beginning. The officers then dragged the bloodied man to the toilet and resumed their beatdown. Volpe was especially brutal in his attack, forcing Abner to the floor while mercilessly kicking him, particularly in his genitals. He also grabbed his testicles forcefully. With the victim's hands cuffed behind his back, he was powerless to defend himself.

Officer Volpe then warned Abner that if he screamed or yelled, he'd be killed before picking up a snapped broomstick. Taking the sharp end of the broken wooden object, he violated Abner. After the horrific rape, which badly damaged Abner internally, Volpe taunted his victim in a sadistic way: he removed the bloodied broomstick and forced it inside of Abner's mouth. He did so with such force that he broke some of the victim's teeth.

Once the officers were done with their twisted abuse and humiliation, they flung Abner into a jail cell and warned him he'd be killed if he spoke of what had just happened to him.

As Abner sat alone, bleeding in his cold cell, Volpe and the other officers involved in the nightclub scuffle earlier in the evening all took themselves to the hospital for the minor injuries they'd received. It was here that Volpe bragged to other officers that he'd "broken a man down" that evening.

It was only over four hours later that Abner was taken to the hospital. For four hours, he'd sat in his blood and excrement, alone and afraid to tell anyone what had happened. When the NYPD did eventually seek medical care for the badly injured man, they didn't take him to the closest hospital; they took him to a hospital four miles away at Coney Island. No reason was given for this, although interestingly, the hospital at Coney Island lacked a trauma center and, subsequently, trauma nurses who could have offered comprehensive aftercare to Abner.

As the surgeons were called in to tend to Abner's extensive internal injuries, the officers who brought him to the hospital would explain them away as occurring from "consensual" sex

Abner had engaged in with another man. Nurse Magalie Laurent wouldn't take the cops' claims at face value. She knew something sinister had happened to Abner, and it certainly wasn't consensual. Magalie took her concerns to the Internal Affairs Bureau at the police department straight away. She also told Abner's family she believed he'd been assaulted and raped while in police custody.

It only took a matter of days for the police report to make the news. The people of New York were stunned at the torture and brutality Abner had endured. When they came to realize it was at the hands of the NYPD, they were horrified. The first newspaper report of the attack included quotes from Abner, taken while he still lay in his hospital bed. He described how the officers stuck a "stick in his rear end," which, as horrific as that quote is, doesn't come close to describing just how barbaric the assault really was.

Abner also described the officers as racially abusing him as they carried out the attack. As a result of the newspaper article, thousands of people marched in protest, causing the Brooklyn Bridge to be shut down.

The police had no choice but to act; the story had rightfully caused outrage. Justin Volpe, Charles Schwarz, Thomas Bruder, and Thomas Wiese were all arrested and charged with assault, attempting to cover it up and denying Abner Louima his constitutional rights. However, the charges against Bruder and Wiese didn't stick.

Schwarz's first trial was deemed unfair, and he was granted a new one. In the end, he was only found guilty of perjury and was handed five years in jail.

Sergeant Michael Bellamo was charged with helping the officers cover up their crime. He was eventually acquitted.

Meanwhile, Abner was having to endure operation after operation to repair the damage he'd sustained to his insides. He was laid up in the hospital for months after the attack.

Justin Volpe's trial took place in 1999, and the disgraced former officer denied all charges put to him. However, he had a change of heart partway through the proceedings and eventually admitted to abusing Abner. The only aspect of the attack he denied was breaking the victim's teeth: he said he didn't hit Abner with the bloodied broomstick after violating him with it. He said it held it close to the man's face but didn't strike him.

In December 1999, Volpe was handed 30 years in jail and ordered to pay $277,495 restitution.

In 2001, Abner was awarded an $8.75 million settlement in a civil suit against the city for the brutality he endured at the hands of the police. Once his legal fees were taken away, he walked away with around $5.8 million. Although a large sum of money, no amount of dollars, no matter how many million, could erase the memories of being so barbarically attacked and violated by those sworn to protect you.

Abner used part of his settlement to set up the Abner Louima Foundation. The charity aims to raise money to build community centers and hospitals in his home country of Haiti. He also used a portion of the funds to invest in property and now lives in Florida with his wife and daughter.

Schwarz was released from jail in 2006 and now works in New York as a carpenter.

Volpe was released from jail early in the spring of 2023.

Talking about Volpe's early release, Abner said he believed his attacker should have served the full sentence he was handed. Although he accepted his abuser had been released, he said, "Let the amount of time he served in jail send a message to police officers all over the country."

Unrequited Hate

In 2019, Ally Kostial was studying business and marketing at the University of Mississippi. The young woman was a popular student who adored "chick flicks", interior design, was passionate about fitness, and spending time with her friends. She wasn't unlike many 21-year-olds, enjoying nights out and spending time at the beach.

She was extremely close with her mother, Cindy, who shared her daughter's love of cooking and passion for interior design.

Ally dreamed of getting married one day and, like a lot of young women, envisioned her future relationship and daydreamed of her perfect wedding. The only problem was that Ally's love interest wasn't so interested in her.

She'd met Brandon Theesfeld in late 2016, but the 22-year-old student refused to settle down with Ally even after almost two years of sporadic dating. After all, he was still young, and his passions included partying and drinking. A committed relationship was not in his near future.

However, he didn't explicitly tell Ally that. He did, however, mistreat her and often simply ignored her calls and texts altogether. Still, Ally adored Brandon and would text him multiple times, sometimes daily, despite his infrequent replies. Ally had told her friends all about Brandon, and it was clear to them that this wasn't the relationship Ally thought it was. It was the definition of unrequited love, though young and naive Ally wasn't able to digest this as the truth. She still thought they were meant to be; Brandon just couldn't see it.

Tellingly, Ally had never introduced Brandon to her friends. He simply hadn't wanted to meet them.

Still, from what Ally's close friends knew about him, they didn't want to meet Brandon, either. He was seen as cruel and unnecessarily mean to Ally. They'd seen some of the messages he'd sent her and would have to comfort their friend as she cried over the uninterested boy. None of her girlfriends could understand why she stuck around, only to be verbally abused by Brandon time and time again.

Ally's friends weren't the only ones with a negative opinion of Brandon. Another student who lived at the same dorm as him would describe him as a rich daddy's boy who acted entitled and was rude, especially to girls. He was described as being "vulgar" toward the opposite sex and bragged that his father had enough money to get him out of any trouble he may find himself in.

In the spring of 2019, Ally took a pregnancy test, which proved to be inconclusive. She sent Brandon the test results, and he made it clear he did not want to be a father. "I will not help at all," he texted Ally, "Just take a pill."

He panicked about what his family, in particular his dad, would think. The Theesfelds were a wealthy family who financed Brandon's existence. Having a baby before graduating could possibly ruin that for him. He was sure his father would cut him off, and he'd have to fend for himself.

Ally blew up Brandon's phone, begging him to at least speak to her. He began ignoring her, which wasn't out of the norm. But, while he was screening her calls, he posted a picture of a gun on social media. This *was* out of the norm, even for someone like Brandon, who often flouted rules.

Eventually, Brandon got back to Ally, who had been anxiously texting him repeatedly. He said he'd meet her. When Ally showed up at the agreed location, Brandon never turned up. Months passed, and Brandon continued to ignore his possibly pregnant on-again-off-again partner.

In one text she sent him that summer, she told him she'd drank a bottle of tequila and two bottles of champagne over the course of a weekend. She then questioned her ability to be a mother. Still, she received the cold shoulder. As summer heated up, Ally tried to convince Brandon to meet her. He eventually agreed, and this time, he showed up.

They met at a campsite close to Sardis Lake. Brandon came fueled by cocaine and alcohol.

The next morning, Ally's roommates were surprised to find she'd not returned home. It wasn't long before Ally's dead body was found, and nine bullets had been pumped into her.

The search for her killer was on. Investigators came to search Ally's dorm room and searched her devices, looking for clues to lead them to her killer. It didn't take long for Brandon to become a suspect; they'd read Ally's messages, and Brandon's name was mentioned by almost every one of Ally's friends. They had trouble finding him, though.

When they did reach him, he said he couldn't come to the station but promised to come by the following Monday for a voluntary interview. He would never show up.

Investigators were then able to obtain an arrest affidavit, which allowed them to start tracking his phone. The tracker showed Brandon making his way to Memphis. A lookout alert was issued for him, and he was quickly picked up at a gas station. His shorts and t-shirt were still blood-stained. The gun found in his vehicle matched the same type that had been used to kill Ally.

Daniel Theesfeld insisted his son would never do such a thing and urged for his boy to be released from police custody.

Ally's subsequent autopsy showed she was not pregnant, making the motive for this murder evaporate into the air. Brandon killed her for a baby that had never existed. He'd never seen conclusive proof she was ever pregnant, yet he took her life out of the fear she was.

Brandon pleaded guilty to first-degree murder. He was sentenced to life in prison without parole. After the sentencing, Brandon's mother, Kerry, took accountability for not knowing her son was struggling with the news of an unwanted pregnancy. If she had known, she said the situation would never have gotten to the tragic point it did.

"We will always pray for the family and friends of Ally Kostial," she added.

She reiterated to parents that it's important to sit down with their children and remind them that there's never anything too bad or complex that they can't talk through with you.

Judy's Law

Burning to death is considered one of the most painful ways to go. The thought of enduring the agonizing trauma of being burned alive is one thing; the idea of the painful aftermath is another thing entirely. For Judith Malinowski, not only did she endure the horror of being set ablaze by her boyfriend, but she spent over 18 months in a hospital bed, clinging to life, wrapped in bandages, her face and body disfigured from the attack.

She lost her ears, hair, fingers, and ability to do anything for herself. Over 90% of her body was covered in either third or fourth-degree burns. She described the lasting pain as being akin to "a thousand hot needles" stabbing her body.

Judy was a young mother whose life hadn't been plain sailing. Born in Ohio in 1983, her childhood was filled with love and laughter, but as Judy entered her teen years, things began to go downhill. The homecoming queen would be diagnosed with ovarian cancer. Judy was a fighter, though, and managed to beat it in her early 20s. The young woman went on to have two children, and she relished her role as a mother.

However, in 2006, she received the devastating news that the cancer had returned.

Judy had to undergo a full hysterectomy, and to deal with the pain afterward, she was prescribed opiates. This was during a time when the USA was dealing with an opiate crisis, with young people becoming addicted to the likes of morphine, hydrocodone, and oxycodone due to misprescribing the addictive drugs. Sadly, Judy was caught up in the epidemic and quickly found herself addicted to opiates.

Thankfully, Judy's family was on hand to help raise her two young children, and for a while, her daughters were taken out of her care completely. Although this undoubtedly caused Judy heartache, she knew she wasn't capable of meeting her children's needs while she struggled to overcome her addiction.

Eventually, Judy's insurance ran out, thus causing her direct line to opiates—her prescription—to be abruptly taken from her. The young mother was desperate, and her desperation caused her to eventually obtain drugs from the streets. It was a bleak period for Judy, though her family didn't once consider turning their backs on her. They understood that recovery wasn't possible until Judy was ready to face the problem and commit to going clean.

With their love and support, Judy finally understood the gravity of the situation she was in. She worked hard to get sober and eventually made leaps and bounds in her bid to get clean.

While she was on the road to health, Judy felt able to reenter the dating pool, and after being contacted by a man named Michael Slager via social media, the pair entered a relationship. After just one date, the two became inseparable. It could appear that Slager "love bombed" Judy, professing his love and adoration early on in order to exert control over her. Certainly, his behavior as the relationship evolved only appeared to get more and more domineering.

Tragically, Slager reintroduced Judy to drugs. This time, though, it was heroin. Naturally, the young mother quickly became addicted. Slager didn't use drugs himself but would acquire heroin daily for his vulnerable girlfriend. The 40-year-old was no stranger to controlling and abusive behavior. His lengthy criminal record included charges of domestic assault, child endangerment, and stalking.

However, by the time Judy realized she'd let a monster into her life, it was too late: she was deep in the throes of addiction—to which Slager was her sole supplier—and she was powerless to release herself from his clutches. It's a toxic cycle that abusers often utilize, making their victims dependent on them.

The relationship was tumultuous. Although Judy was using again, she wanted to be clean and away from the suppressive and toxic relationship. She made multiple attempts to get free of her abuser, calling 911 over domestic abuse incidents. Sadly, Slager wasn't removed from the property at any time. Judy's mother believes that the authorities simply brushed her off as an addict and didn't pay much heed to her complaints.

If they had examined Slager's criminal history more thoroughly, they would have noticed a sinister pattern repeating itself.

It had only taken Slager a few short months to drag Judy from sobriety to rock bottom, and again, her family remained on hand, waiting for her to return to them. By August 2015, she'd had enough and was adamant she wanted to get clean. She booked herself back into rehab. She'd only met Slager around April time, but he'd done untold damage to her in the months in between.

On August 2, Judy found herself in yet another heated argument with Slager. The pair were at a gas station, and the interaction saw Judy throw the remnants of her soda at Slager. His response wasn't to leave the area. Instead, he doused Judy in gasoline. As horrendous as this is, it wasn't enough for the rage-filled man. He headed back to his truck and retrieved his lighter.

It took him 30 seconds to get to the truck, find his lighter, and return to Judy. In those seconds, he had the opportunity to calm down, rationalize the situation, and take stock of what he was about to do. Slager chose not to do this and basked in his rage instead. He was hell-bent on causing damage to Judy.

When he returned to a gas-soaked Judy, she realized what he was about to do. She begged and pleaded with him not to set her alight. He didn't listen, and Judy's entire body was ablaze in moments. The attacker simply looked on at the untold, irreversible damage he'd just done to the young mother.

All the while, Judy was screaming for help, begging her aggressor to put the fire out. Again, he merely stood, gawping at the result of his actions.

There was an abundance of passersby who saw the horrifying sight of Judy alight and called 911. As they approached Slager to see what had happened, he began telling his version of events: that he'd accidentally set her on fire after they were sharing a cigarette.

The ambulance arrived, and first responders all thought the same thing: *this woman isn't going to make it*.

However, Judy proved health workers wrong: She fought to stay alive. She was clinging on—just.

Meanwhile, the police got involved and reviewed the CCTV footage of a nearby ATM machine that caught the whole episode on video. Not only that, unbeknownst to Slager, some people had witnessed firsthand his attack on Judy. However, Slager still lied to the police, insisting it was an accident.

Judy was comatose and unable to give her version of events. Nobody was hopeful she'd come around. Even if she did, it was unlikely she'd have much memory of the traumatic event.

As determined authorities worked on building a case, Judy lay in a coma for months, her life hanging by a thread.

Officers were unsure of what to charge Slager with. They were expecting Judy to pass away any day now and didn't want to charge the assailant with anything less than he'd done. They wanted to get him for murder. Assistant Prosecutor Warren Edwards would later admit that he and his team found themselves delaying the case so they could charge Slager with Judy's murder. That would ensure the death penalty was on the table for the attacker.

However, a miracle happened: Judy woke up. Just as miraculous was the fact that she remembered the attack. Judy's version of events, unsurprisingly, matched what the CCTV depicted and what witnesses told the police.

Still, Judy was in immense pain. So much pain that she struggled to put it into words. Recalling the day she was set alight, she remembered thinking that she was about to die and prayed that her sins be forgiven and that her children would be taken care of.

Her pain would continue when she awoke from her coma. She endured over 50 surgeries to try and repair her damaged skin, which often proved to be too far damaged for the surgery to be successful.

Because Judy hadn't died, the prosecution was unable to proceed with their anticipated murder charge and instead charged Michael Slager with aggravated arson and felonious assault. The heavily tattooed man was handed 11 years behind bars, which was the maximum the judge could give out.

As you would imagine, Judy and the Malinowski family were beyond disheartened by the light sentence. Judy would never live a normal life again. Certainly, she'd never live to see her children grow up and make lives of their own. Judy and her medical team knew it wasn't a matter of *if* she succumbed to her injuries, but *when* she succumbed to them. She'd already survived 18 months after the attack, which was 18 more than anybody had expected.

She was on borrowed time, while Slager would be out of jail before he was 50 and free to start life anew. It simply wasn't fair.

The lack of justice offered to Judy made her fight for the laws to be changed. From her hospital bed, she fought for the law to be more strict with attackers who disfigured and maimed their victims. She knew she didn't have long left, but wanted to make a change while she could. After all, she was leaving two young girls behind, and the idea that something like this could happen to them terrified Judy. Thinking that the perpetrators of such attacks could get off so lightly fueled Judy's will to have the law amended.

Prosecutors felt the anger of injustice, too. They knew Judy was going to pass as a result of her injuries and that the attacker wouldn't be justly punished. So, they decided to preemptively ensure that Slager was punished for killing Judy whenever she eventually succumbed to her injuries.

Judy was deteriorating rapidly, and her pain medication was the only thing keeping her conscious. Although it barely touched the sides of her pain, it ensured she could speak with family members and deal with the police when they wanted to speak with her. Just over 18 months after the attack, the police came to her with an idea: they wanted to take a recorded testimony from her while she was still alive. That way, when the day came, they'd attempt to overturn Slager's paltry sentence and get him tried for murder.

There was just one problem: Judy's requirement of high-strength medication could be used as a way to discredit her. So, they asked her if she would be comfortable drastically decreasing her dosage to make her testimony. She agreed despite the blatant agony it would cause. She wanted to make sure she saw justice through until the end.

The resulting three-hour video—which is a heartbreaking glimpse into just how much pain Judy was in—offered a terrifying recount of the events that took place the day she was attacked. She described how Slager's eyes turned black as he set her alight and ignored her pleas for help. "Just stop," she pleaded. "I'll go with you," she reasoned with Slager to no avail. Before she knew it, every inch of her was in flames.

Judy recounted how some of the gasoline had run down her throat as she writhed in pain. "That burnt really bad," she said. She told the camera that Slager was evil, got her addicted to heroin, and abused her prior to dousing her in gasoline that day. She told of her attempts to flee the relationship, even calling the police, who did nothing.

Struggling to inhale deeply, her sentences broken with gasps, Judy somehow mustered the strength and will to finish her testimony. Despite the agony she was in, Judy made it clear she didn't want Slager to receive the death penalty. Instead, she wanted him to find religion and become a better person.

Five months later, on June 27, 2017, Judy yielded to her injuries. She left behind her two young daughters, who would be taken care of by her family.

Slager was retried for murder, and the tape Judy recorded was played at his trial. This time, he pleaded guilty and was sentenced to life in prison.

Two months after she died, Legislators passed what was named "Judy's Law." The amended law saw attackers who disfigure their victims receive up to six years longer on their sentences.

The prosecutor in this case would later say that it was the first murder case he'd been a part of where he'd been able to meet the victim.

An Incorrect Number

On September 27, 1992, 19-year-old Californian Jennifer Asbenson was standing waiting for the bus to work. Public transport wasn't always reliable, and the bus was running late, which meant Jennifer was going to clock in late. When a good Samaritan pulled up beside her and offered her a lift, she said yes. This would usually be against her better judgment, but she was in a pinch.

The man who picked her up was chatty and friendly, though it was clear he'd taken a liking to the young woman. As he dropped her off at her workplace, he asked her for her number. She jotted it down for him and handed it to him. Only, it was fake. Jennifer wasn't interested in the man but didn't feel comfortable saying no to him while he was driving her to work.

Plus, what were the chances she'd ever bump into him again?

When the young woman finished her shift hours later and exited the building, the man was there, waiting in his car. It was like he hadn't left since dropping her off. He had, though, and he'd tried the number Jennifer had given him, perhaps getting the feeling it might have been fake.

Instead of moving on from it, the man wanted revenge. He knew where Jennifer worked and was going to make sure she paid for humiliating him.

When he spotted Jennifer leaving work, he again offered her a lift. She said thank you, but no thank you, and said she was going to get the bus home. However, the man was friendly and managed to put her at ease. Jennifer was all too aware she'd given him a fake number just hours earlier, but she knew he probably hadn't tried to call it yet, so she hopped in the car.

The friendly man's demeanor didn't change as he drove to her house, and the conversation flowed.

Then, without warning, the man switched from friendly to terrifying in a split second. His once-grinning face was replaced with wide-eyed anger, and he pulled a gun on Jennifer before pulling over. With one hand, he grabbed her hair; with the other, he pointed the gun in her face. He called her multiple derogatory names before demanding to know why she gave him a fake number.

It seems the fake number wasn't a clear enough answer for the man: Jennifer wasn't interested and felt too uncomfortable to say so at the time. So, he bound her hands together behind her back and began cutting away at her clothes. He aggressively tried to kiss her before trying to rape her. He was physically unable to do so, after which the terrified woman screamed at her attacker to just kill her and be done with it. She also called him a coward at one point, causing the brute to choke her until she almost lost consciousness.

Once his hands got too sore, he beat his victim and bit her neck hard enough to draw blood and leave an impression. After the sustained attack, he bundled her into the trunk of the car and sped off. Jennifer was aware this man was about to kill her. However, she was a fighter.

While trapped in the trunk, she managed to work the lock until it sprung the lid open. The car was traveling fast, but it didn't matter: this was Jennifer's one shot at making it out of her certain death situation. She flung herself from the trunk with all her might and rolled down the road. The manic driver didn't stop despite it being obvious his victim had escaped. He sped off.

Jennifer, half-naked, ran through the streets to find safety, which appeared to be nowhere around. Out of nowhere, her attacker reappeared with a machete, and he began chasing her around the streets. The terrified young woman finally managed to flag down a truck that had two burly marines inside. This caused the big, tough attacker to retreat to his vehicle and race away.

Jennifer had made it out of the clutches of a maniac. However, there was not enough evidence to capture the assailant, aside from the nasty bite mark she had. Jennifer had no clue at the time, but she was the only person who survived an encounter with serial killer Andrew Urdiales.

Urdiales was born in the mid-60s, and little is known about his childhood. He finished high school in Illinois before joining the Marines. In his early 20s, he committed his first murder in

California, stabbing student Robbin Brandley to death. It was a brutal, sustained attack that saw Robbin endure over 40 stab wounds.

His next attack occurred two years later, in the summer of 1988. His weapon of choice was now a gun, and he shot Julie McGhee dead with a pistol. Due to the completely different MOs, it's unlikely officers would have connected the murders. Later that year, he struck twice more: once in San Diego, killing Mary Ann Wells, 31, and again in Palm Springs, killing Tammie Erwin, 18. Tammie wasn't found until 1989.

Urdiales laid low for the next two years, but after he was discharged from the Marines, he was free to roam the streets as he pleased. Despite having a base in Chicago, his newfound freedom saw him return to his old stomping ground of California regularly.

It would be here in 1992 that Jennifer Asbenson would have the utter misfortune of crossing paths with him. It appears her surviving spooked Urdiales, who knew she could identify him. As a result, he refrained from killing for three years. However, by 1995, he was back at it. He killed Denise Maney after coercing her into his car under the guise of sex work.

He would branch away from killing in California for his next murders. In 1996, he killed 25-year-old Laura Ulyaki in Indiana and 21-year-old Cassandra Corum, and 22-year-old Lynn Huber in Illinois.

Despite his crimes and clearly violent temper, Urdiales had no real run-ins with the law until, in late 1996, he was arrested for carrying an unlicensed gun. He was allowed to walk free at the time, but he was hauled back in by early 1997 when investigators thought they could connect his gun to a number of crimes.

Once Urdiales was in police custody, he confessed to all the murders he'd committed. Even before the ballistics tests had come back, the killer admitted everything to the police. Once the ballistic results came back, it was confirmed that his confessions were true.

Despite Urdiales' quick confession, his case dragged on for years. The big concern for law enforcement and politicians was whether or not he should be sentenced to death. On May 30, 2002, almost five years after he'd been arrested, Urdiales was handed the death penalty. Jennifer Asbenson, his sole surviving victim, was able to testify against him at the trial.

Despite being sentenced to the lethal injection, he'd never meet his maker this way. In late 2018, Urdiales was found unresponsive in his cell. The 54-year-old had hung himself.

Not Jeremy Again

For at least the past two decades, Floridian Jeremy Dewitte has been busy impersonating police officers. As well as dressing up as a cop—complete with dummy gun and badge—he's also been on a crime rampage, involving offenses as serious as sexual battery.

The serial criminal would wear a police uniform and patrol the streets of Florida from a young age. The wannabe cop quite literally ruined any career he would have had in law enforcement after being caught pretending to be an officer. His first arrest for this odd crime came in 1998 when he was still a teenager. Dewitte was pretending to be an undercover cop at a gas station, though he wasn't very sophisticated in carrying out his ruse.

After filling his car full of gas, the teenager was able to convince the cashier that he was a plain-clothed police officer and that he would return the following day to make payment for the $14 gas bill. However, the young man was thoughtless enough to give the cashier his real name and actual home address.

So, when he didn't come back the following day to pay his debt, the gas station attendant contacted the police. They knew exactly where to find the young man.

Perhaps due to his age, his antics weren't seen as overly troublesome at the time. Law enforcement may have seen Dewitte's actions as someone simply trying to evade paying for gas. Still, the teenager was charged with stealing the gas and impersonating an officer, though he received little in the way of punishment.

Dewitte's strange and dangerous behavior would only escalate as he got older.

What started as the young man posing as an undercover officer soon evolved into him wearing a uniform almost identical to the local police force. He became bolder as the years passed, as did his crimes.

By 2001, he was arrested again for impersonating a police officer. Now 21, Dewitte had kitted his car out to look like an unmarked police vehicle, complete with a radio and flashing lights. He was acting suspiciously at a local mall, telling individuals he was there to snare thieves. One witness was so suspicious of the "undercover cop" that they called the real officers, who quickly arrested him.

Again, Dewitte was released, but he would find himself in trouble again in 2003. Yet again, he'd been caught impersonating a police officer. This time, though, he'd serve time behind bars for his repeated breaking of the law. He was handed a two-year prison sentence, but by 2005, he was back at it again.

This time, his crime wasn't for impersonating a police officer; it was for the sexual battery of a young girl. Little was publicized about this, but online records show the victim was between 12 and 15 years of age. The crime was described as "lewd or lascivious battery." For this, he was jailed for one year.

When Dewitte was released, he'd run in with the law again. He refused to register as a sex offender, which was part of his release conditions. His failure to do so saw him hauled back to jail. He was back on the streets by 2011, though, as you've perhaps guessed by now, wouldn't stay off law enforcement's radar for long.

Dewitte would set up his own business, Metro State Vehicle Protection Services, which saw him escort funeral processions. However, he would do so in full police attire. He would use his motorcycle and fake police getup to direct traffic, stop people from crossing the street, and stop cars for no apparent reason. In fact, much of this was captured from his own helmet footage. He would speed between traffic under the ruse of being a police officer darting to the scene of a crime. In reality, he wasn't speeding to get anywhere. It was all part of his charade.

There's footage of this online, and it makes for alarming—and, at times, almost comical—viewing. The phony cop would scream at confused drivers, force them to pull over and scold them for made-up infractions. One phrase may come to mind when viewing this: superiority complex.

Astonishingly, much of this footage was published online by Dewitte himself.

Sadly, many of the people Dewitte chastised believed he truly was a law enforcement officer. They had no reason not to: his bike, attire, helmet, radio, and badge all led them to believe he was legitimate. Besides, rarely do you find a grown man all dressed up in a police uniform, raging at drivers and trying to redirect them.

The story only gets stranger.

By mid-2019, he had a full funeral escort service with 18 vehicles (all made to look like police cruisers) and a handful of employees who, like Dewitte, basked in dressing like a cop and acting like a law enforcement officer. The team was only licensed to escort funeral cars in permitted areas, but the small team took their roles seriously. More than escorting funeral cars, they attempted to maintain law and order on the roads. Oftentimes, they'd do more harm than good.

In Dewitte's body cam footage, he can be heard swearing at other motorists and, in one instance, ironically scolding an off-duty sheriff. When the sheriff questioned Dewitte's legitimacy, he rounded up his Metro State Vehicle Protection Services employees to chase the man away.

Twice in 2019, Dewitte had run-ins with the law over his persistent impersonations of police officers.

In the footage inline, you can see one of Dewitte's arrests. When the (real) police officer gets out of their patrol car to apprehend the fake officer, you can hear him say, "Oh God, not him again... It's Jeremy." Dewitte had become something of a nuisance to the Osceola County police force, and most officers had come to know of the serial criminal.

In February 2021, Dewitte made an appearance on an American talk show to deny claims that he was a serial police officer impersonator. He also showed the host his bike to show it wasn't the same as a police bike.

In March 2021, he was caught impersonating an officer yet again.

This time, his sentence was much harsher: not only did he get handed a year and a half in jail, but his driving license was suspended for six months.

As you can imagine, upon his release, it wasn't long before Dewitte was in trouble again. This time, it was because he'd refused to take down the videos he'd uploaded online showing him directing traffic and yelling at motorists. However, Dewitte insisted he was unable to access his account and disable it.

The persistent criminal was arrested again in 2023 for insurance fraud and in the spring of 2024 for not updating vehicle ownership.

Florida's police departments seem all too aware of Dewitte, although this doesn't seem to trouble the man, who's now in his 40s. He doesn't seem to mind the negative attention his actions bring, nor do his countless arrests and time in jail put him off donning his police officer uniform.

Time will tell if Dewitte will be in trouble with the law again. Still, he remains Florida's most infamous sham police officer.

Who Ended Ellen's Life?

The following case isn't a crime case per se; rather, it was never ruled as a criminal case. But the circumstances of Ellen Greenberg's death are so extraordinary many people refuse to believe her death wasn't a murder.

This poses an unusual question: who ended Ellen's life? Was it Ellen herself or a killer who still evades justice?

On January 26, 2011, the 27-year-old teacher was found lying dead in her Philadelphia apartment. Her death was ruled to be a tragic suicide. However, the facts of the case don't necessarily match with the cause of death: she died of 20 stab wounds. Still, investigators decided her death was self-inflicted.

Naturally, Ellen's family struggled to accept the ruling. *Surely she couldn't have stabbed herself 20 times*?

More than this, some of her wounds were on her back in places she would have been unable to reach. When the Greenberg family ruminated on Ellen's final days alive, they considered her mood. She wasn't low, nor did she seem unhappy. She was her usual self, which was vivacious and lively.

She mentioned that work was particularly busy and that she felt stressed, but aside from that, nothing seemed out of sorts.

So, not only did the scene of the crime suggest her death was caused by someone else, but there were zero signs from Ellen that she was planning on ending her life. To those who knew her, she was in a happy relationship, enjoyed her job at an elementary school, and looked forward to having a family of her own one day.

On January 26, 2011, Ellen was sent home from work due to a worsening snowstorm in her hometown of Philadelphia, Pennsylvania. To avoid getting stranded at the school, she headed out just after lunchtime, stopping for gas before getting home around early afternoon.

Ellen lived with her fiance, Samuel Goldberg, who greeted her when she arrived home. He was an avid gym-goer who rarely skipped a day, so later that afternoon, he headed out and spent an hour or so pumping iron. When he returned, he found their apartment door wouldn't open. It was locked from the inside, meaning there was no way for him to use a key. He knocked and banged on the door to no avail. He knew Ellen was inside.

Goldberg sent text after text urging his fiance to let him in. "Hello," he said, "Open the door." More messages that said more or less the same thing were ignored. "You better have an excuse," he wrote, now angry at being locked out of his home for seemingly no reason. His other option was to head to the building security office and ask them to bust the door open for him. They refused.

Now Goldberg had one final idea: to break the door down himself. He did so, charging into the apartment to see what Ellen was playing at.

She was sitting against the kitchen cabinets, a knife protruding from her chest. She had multiple stab wounds. Goldberg called 911 immediately, but there was no saving Ellen. The 20 stab wounds around her head, neck, and torso saw to that. Ten of them were at the back of her head.

"I think she hit her head," Goldberg told the 911 operator. "She stabbed herself... she fell on a knife! There is a knife sticking out of her heart."

The police arrived and felt it was pretty obvious that this gruesome scene was a murder. But then, the facts didn't quite add up.

All the surface evidence suggested Ellen was on her own when she died. The knife was tested for the DNA of the perpetrator. The only DNA on there was Ellen's. Had someone furiously attacked her—which is what it certainly looked like—it was strange that Ellen didn't have any defensive wounds. The security team didn't notice anyone untoward or suspicious entering the building. Nothing was missing from Ellen and Goldberg's apartment, either.

Even stranger, the apartment door had been locked from the inside. Whoever did this would have had to have been locked inside the apartment with Ellen when she was found. There was only one escape—off the balcony, which was six floors high. Plus, the balcony was covered in fresh snow with not a footprint in sight.

As unlikely as it seemed at first glance, investigators were leaning toward the idea that Ellen had carried out this barbaric attack on herself. All 20 stab wounds were determined to have been carried out by her. Even though some of the wounds were absent of blood, suggesting they'd been inflicted after she'd died.

To prop up the theory that Ellen had done this to herself, investigators began looking into her recent history for signs that she was unhappy. Sure enough, she was on two separate medications for anxiety. She was also seeing a psychiatrist, to whom she'd told of her feelings of worry and stress surrounding her career.

A deeper look into the medications Ellen was taking showed that both drugs had been known, in rare instances, to cause suicidal ideations.

This premise was put to the Greenberg family, who rebuffed the idea that Ellen had killed herself. Not only did they disagree that she had notions of ending her life, but they pointed to the murder scene itself. "That's rage," her mother Sandra would say. "She did not do that to herself."

Certainly, one would think that it would have been impossible for her to inflict a stab wound on herself after she'd died, which one of the lesions was. Then, there was the final stab puncture to the heart, where the knife was placed when she was found. That would make it two posthumous injuries that Ellen—apparently—inflicted upon herself. To say the

Greenberg family was confused is an understatement. They were dumbfounded that the authorities weren't seeing their side: that this was clearly a homicide.

The Greenberg family pointed to other pieces of evidence they felt were being overlooked. Ellen had over ten bruises spanning her arms, torso, and one of her legs. Some bruises were older and in the process of healing; some were still fairly fresh. Either way, the Greenberg family felt the number of welts Ellen had across her body suggested she'd been the victim of abuse in the weeks prior to her untimely death.

Her dad, Joshua, felt like somebody didn't want Ellen's abuse to become public knowledge. As a result, she was murdered, he suggested. The Greenbergs feel as if the death of Ellen was brushed off too quickly as a suicide, despite the evidence they say shows otherwise.

They say the investigation was flawed from the offset.

As of writing, Joshua and Sandra Greenberg are still seeking justice for Ellen, and they want the case to be reopened and looked into thoroughly. However, Joshua believes that the lack of urgency to find Ellen's killer is because there are depths to the story that nobody wants to dig into.

As is, the case remains closed: it's still determined that Ellen killed herself.

As you can imagine, cases like this cause so-called armchair detectives (a term I occasionally use for myself) to delve into the facts available and try to make sense of them. Because this case is so unique and perplexing, even a former FBI agent has spoken out and professed her belief that Ellen's death most certainly wasn't at her own hands. Former agent Jennifer Coffindaffer's eye of suspicion is directed at Samuel Goldberg.

One aspect of the case she can't agree with is Goldberg's claim that, after going to the gym, he broke down the apartment door when he was unable to get inside. As Jennifer can tell from the pictures of the busted door, the frame and door don't have enough damage to suggest someone's had to smash it open.

This case continues to divide people on what they think truly happened to Ellen: some claim the suicide ruling is entirely plausible, and others suggest killing yourself in that manner is impossible.

Sadly, the one person who can tell us the truth is no longer with us.

Ellen's ex-fiance was never arrested over her death and now lives in New York with his family.

Stalker Mom

I read a sad quote not too long ago: *a mother is often her daughter's first bully*.

This case is quite literally an embodiment of that quote.

Kendra Gail Licari was a mother of one who appeared to dote on her teenage daughter. When Kendra's daughter came to her in 2021 to tell her she was being bullied, the mother was supportive and empathetic. She comforted her daughter, who showed her numerous text messages from her bullies.

The cruel messages told the young girl to kill herself, among other shocking taunts. The texts weren't just directed at the girl, either. The harasser also began texting the teenager's boyfriend, again vomiting hate to the innocent boy.

Between Kendra's daughter and her boyfriend, the youngsters were getting multiple texts each day. When it all got too much, and the texts became increasingly obscene, Kendra went to the police to report her daughter's cyberbully, whoever they may have been.

Kendra would join forces with her daughter's boyfriend's mother to help track down the sick individual sending the cruel messages to their children. Kendra was a mainstay in her daughter's school in Michigan, coaching the girl's basketball team. She would be sure to keep an ear out for anything that may lead them to the persistent bully.

Why would anyone ever consider the horrific truth? That the bully was the victim's mother?

Still, Kendra Licari went to greater lengths than just creating fake social media profiles to taunt her child and her boyfriend. She took great measures to cover her tracks and ensure her twisted secret never got out.

In December 2021, Kendra and her daughter went to the school to report the never-ending bullying. Beal City Schools opened their own investigation, leading them to call the police over the messages. After all, the texts and posts aimed at Kendra's daughter weren't just a bit mean; they were downright vile. The frequency and malignancy of the messages meant they couldn't simply close the case.

After all, whatever teenager carrying out this campaign of terror was clearly unhinged, and who knew if their demented behavior would escape from messages to real-life attacks?

The local police were also stumped. They couldn't trace the source of the messages, and even their computer crime team struggled to make any break in the case. There was one last resort, though: the FBI.

Usually, the FBI wouldn't step in on a case like this, but the perpetrator was continuously outsmarting law enforcement. They had to be stopped before something irreversible happened. After all, the hateful messages were only getting worse, and law enforcement couldn't just drop the investigation because they'd failed to pinpoint the culprit.

Kendra had been using software to hide her location and used multiple numbers with different area codes. She also implied that her daughter's friends were sending the sickening messages. However, Kendra must have realized the net was closing in once the FBI was on the case.

And she'd have been right. They managed to trace the real IP address of the person who was sending the messages. They were sent from Kendra Licari's computer.

Kendra was arrested and presented with almost 350 pages of evidence. She quickly confessed that she was her daughter's bully.

Even though investigators already knew that Kendra was the culprit, for her to admit it still came as a shock. After all, what mother would send her daughter cruel messages, some of which urged the teen to end her own life?

The full contents of the messages have never been made public, aside from the ones where Kendra urged her child to harm herself. Still, at Kendra's trial in 2023, the judge commented that he couldn't imagine why any mother would say such disturbing things to their child. Since Kendra admitted to everything, there was no jury trial, meaning her child was spared from giving evidence.

Despite the teenager being beyond hurt after finding out her mother was her bully all along, she wanted the judge to be lenient with his sentencing. In spite of the horrible things her mother had done the past few years, she still loved her. Plus, she didn't want to be responsible for sending her mother to jail.

The teenage boy who'd also received hateful messages from Kendra felt completely different, as did his mother, who felt betrayed and duped by the mother. They wanted her to serve time in jail, to give her time to think about the disturbing things she'd done, as well as to separate her from her daughter for a period of time.

No motive was offered for why Kendra felt the urge to cyberbully her child. The prosecution suggested that the mother wanted to feel needed by her daughter and unusually referred to it as a case of "Cyber Munchausen Syndrome."

Kendra was tearful and appeared remorseful throughout the trial. She told the judge that if she could erase everything, she would. She said she is left with overwhelming shame and embarrassment over what she did, and her defense argued that psychiatric reports suggested Kendra was suffering from mental illness.

Still, the judge decided that the only option was to impose a prison sentence. Kendra was given jail time and ordered to attend parenting classes. She was sent to Michigan's Special Alternative Incarceration Women's Facility. She can't be released until the end of 2024 at the earliest.

Pray With Me

Eve Carson was a lively, vivacious, yet studious 22-year-old who studied political science at the University of North Carolina at Chapel Hill.

The young girl was the epitome of an academic. Among many other things, she was student body president, a member of the Phi Beta Kappa honor society, and had been hand-selected to take part in a four-year leadership development program. Eve did not take her education for granted but rather grabbed it with both hands. She was also a kind-hearted young woman, traveling abroad to volunteer and also spent time tutoring middle school students.

In the spring of 2008, she wasn't far off graduating. Her reputation had preceded her, and Eve had managed to secure a job offer with a consultancy company before she'd even graduated.

This would never materialize. On March 5, 2008, she was killed.

If we rewind to March 4, it was a day like any other for Eve. She had attended a sports game with some friends but left the party early to go back to her place and study. Eve studied until the early hours, and at around 3:30 am, she headed out to her car to grab something.

Little did she know, some dangerous individuals were lurking in the darkness, looking for their prey.

22-year-old Demario James Atwater and 17-year-old Laurence Alvin Lovette Jr were out looking for someone to rob. The evening prior, they'd had a discussion and decided to get as much money as they could by force. By unfortunate happenstance, they made a choice to walk onto Eve's street, and at the same time, she chose to retrieve something from her vehicle.

Atwater and Lovette were no strangers to breaking the law. Both were on probation at the time and had extensive criminal records for breaking and entering, assault, robbery, and possessing a firearm, among other things. It was only a matter of time before their crimes escalated to something more extreme.

The serial criminals captured Eve as she entered her car and forced her into the back seat. Atwater sat next to the terrified woman, holding a gun to her temple. Lovette drove the car to various ATMs, where they used Eve's card to withdraw varying amounts of money.

The pair didn't seem bothered about being captured; Lovette was caught clear as day on the ATM CCTV since he was the one who collected the cash.

As she was being driven from ATM to ATM, Eve pleaded with her captors to let her go. She told them that they didn't have to kill her; they could take all the money she had and take her car if they just set her free. She was trying to appeal to their human side to no avail.

So, Eve began to pray.

Atwater and Lovette, after collecting as much money as they could, drove their terrified victim to a desolate area not far from her campus. They forced her out of the car and into the woodland. By this point, Eve knew what her fate was. She asked Atwater and Lovette to pray with her.

They didn't.

They shot her instead. Four times in various places on her torso. She lay on the cold, damp woodland floor, blood spilling from her wounds. She wasn't dead; she was still breathing. At this point, she could've been saved. But, aware she was still alive, Atwater retrieved a shotgun and shot her point blank in the head. Heartbreakingly, the shotgun shell passed through her hand as she held it up in defense. She knew exactly what was coming.

Callous Atwater and Lovette didn't care; they'd got what they wanted. A measly few hundred dollars for an innocent girl's life.

Unbeknown to the killers, the shots had been heard by those who lived nearby, and the police were called. They found Eve Carson's body just after 5 am that morning, less than two hours after she'd been abducted. Her car was later found abandoned.

It didn't take long before the investigators found some solid leads. After all, the culprits were caught on CCTV driving around in their victim's car, and Lovette's face was captured perfectly on the ATM cameras.

The killer duo were hauled in and charged with first-degree murder. Law enforcement also charged them with their other spate of crimes that night: robbery, kidnapping, carjacking, and possessing weapons.

Both were handed life in jail without the possibility of parole. Despite Lovette being only 17 at the time he carried out the crimes, the chance of parole was taken away from him.

Even after her untimely death, Eve is still earning achievements; she was awarded the most outstanding woman in the senior class by the University of North Carolina. In addition, the university has founded a scholarship in her name geared toward out-of-state students. They also built the Eve Carson Garden.

Eve did so much in her short life; even if Atwater and Lovette live to be 100, they won't be able to compete with the positive impact Eve had on the world. Hopefully, their time behind bars has allowed the pair—who are now men—to comprehend just how barbaric and senseless their murder of Eve Carson was.

Talk Show Terror

The 90s was the "golden age" for talk shows. The scandalous and often unseemly topics for the show were often headlined at the bottom of the TV screen. "I've been sleeping with your dad" was a surprisingly frequent one. "You're not the biological father," was another. A particularly memorable one is, "Your son can't be mine; he's ginger."

At the time, we found shows like this to be a warped source of humor. Much of the time, we couldn't believe the characters we saw on screen were real. Some talk shows, particularly the ones that would end in violence and brawls, felt scripted. Still, for me and many others in the 90s, talk shows were a guilty pleasure. Now, it would be seen as exploitative.

This next case will go some way toward proving that not all talk shows are scripted. For Scott Amedure, the reason he went on national television was very real: to confess to his friend he had a crush on him. The only obstacle in the way was that Jonathan Schmitz was straight. However, Scott felt this was the moment when he could spill his secret. If Schmitz rejected him, so be it; it would give them something to laugh about later.

Scott's talk show of choice was Jenny Jones, and the theme of "secret crush" fitted his situation perfectly. He had no idea his choice to air his feelings this way would end in his murder.

Scott was born in Pittsburgh, Pennsylvania in 1963. His upbringing was typical for the time. His mother was a homemaker, and his father drove trucks for a living. The

Amedure family would eventually move to Michigan, though Scott's parents would break up not long after the move. However, Scott was on the verge of adulthood and would leave high school to join the Air Force.

His three years with the Air Force weren't easy; Scott dealt with substance abuse problems and would wind up in toxic, abusive relationships. By this point, he had come out, and life in the Army was no longer what Scott wanted. He returned to Michigan and ended up working in bars, which he loved. Scott was sociable and outgoing, and bartending catered to his extroverted side.

It enabled Scott to meet new people and make new friends, of which he already had plenty. The kind-hearted man was a prominent member of the local community and often offered help or shelter to those in need, specifically those with AIDS-related complications. At the time, the virus was still highly misunderstood, but Scott was there to offer his support when only a select few would.

In addition to having a bustling social life and enjoying his job, Scott loved nothing more than sitting in front of the TV and catching up on his talk shows. At the time, the shows were known for making people confront one another and hash out their differences in front of a paying audience.

Watching Jennifer Jones' show gave Scott an idea: he had been crushing on his friend Jonathan Schmitz. He would take him on the show and confess his feelings to him there.

On March 6, 1995, that's just what he did. Schmitz was invited on the show by producers who only told him he had a secret admirer. They didn't disclose the gender but advised him they could be male or female. Schmitz asserts that the producers heavily suggested the admirer was female, so he agreed to go on the show.

The segment was undeniably awkward.

Scott sat on stage with his friend Donna and told the host and the audience about his secret crush on his straight friend. When Schmitz was brought on stage, the atmosphere was dicey, to say the least. Scott and Schmitz embraced one another and sat down, with Schmitz clearly puzzled about what was going on. With there just being Scott and Donna on the stage, it was clear one of them was his secret admirer.

It slowly dawned on Schmitz that it was Scott who was harboring feelings for him.

Jenny then told the perplexed guest who his covert crush was. At first glance, Schmitz took the revelation in good humor, although he stated he was straight, so nothing would come of the infatuation.

When the show wrapped filming, one of Scott's friends would say that he and Schmitz went out for drinks. The friend also suggested that Scott and Schmitz would have a sexual encounter after drinking.

Then, three days after the pair had been on the talk show, Scott would leave what would be described as a "suggestive" note in Schmitz's mailbox. Schmitz was incensed. Fuelled by rage, he drove to an ATM, withdrew a wad of cash, used it to buy a shotgun, and then made his way to Scott's home. At no point along this journey did Schmitz's anger subside. He was angry at his friend for leaving the note, perhaps because it was somewhere as public as his mailbox.

We have to remember this was 1995; homosexuality was seen as shameful by many. Talk shows would use homosexuality as a scandalous headline to draw an audience. Being gay was oftentimes dangerous, thus causing those who perhaps felt attracted to the same sex to violently reject their feelings. It could be this is what happened to Schmitz.

He angrily drove to Scott's and confronted him about leaving the note. When he demanded to know if Scott was responsible for writing and leaving the note in his mailbox, Scott smiled. This served to turn Schmitz from incensed to murderous. He went back to his car, pulled out his newly bought shotgun, and pumped two shots into Scott.

Schmitz immediately called 911 and confessed what he'd done. The police arrived at the crime scene and quickly apprehended the killer.

His trial began the following year, and although Schmitz still maintained he was Scott's killer, he would use "gay panic" as his defense. In a nutshell, the defense strategy asserts that the individual charged with a violent crime against a homosexual (or bisexual) person had lost all control due to being subjected to unwanted sexual advances. This defense strategy is still used in a number of US states, although many have now banned the "gay panic" defense.

In 1996, Schmitz was convicted of second-degree murder and handed 25 to 50 years in jail. He appealed the conviction, which was overturned. However, in 1999, he was re-trialed and was again found guilty of murder and ordered to serve his sentence.

In the aftermath of the case—which garnered a lot of attention at the time due to how unique it was—many people laid blame at the talk show for facilitating the murder. If the show had been forthcoming with Schmitz about the identity of his secret admirer, perhaps he would never have gone on the show, saving Scott from the deadly aftermath.

The Amedure family filed a negligence lawsuit against the talk show and the various TV studios involved in airing it. The bereft family alleged that the producers purposefully ambushed Schmitz with Scott's revelation, not considering the possible violent consequences. The jury awarded the Amedure family over $25,000,000, though this decision would be reversed shortly thereafter, and the talk show was found not liable for Jonathan Schmitz's actions.

Schmitz was released from jail in 2017.

Scott's brother Frank didn't welcome the news. He told the press that he wasn't certain that his brother's killer had truly learned his lesson. Frank said he hoped Schmitz had changed and freed himself from his homophobia but wasn't overly confident that this was the case.

Schmitz has been quiet since his release and hasn't been in trouble with the law. We can only hope that Frank's reservations aren't true and that Schmitz walked out of jail a changed man for the better.

You Are The Company You Keep

Teenage friendships are intense, particularly for young girls. When you're in the throes of a young friendship, you can feel like it's the both of you against the world. You can't imagine ever falling out and not being in one another's lives. Anyone who tries to get in the way of the friendship is quickly shut down.

For teens Pauline Parker and Juliet Hulme, their passionate friendship would be taken to murderous levels to protect it. They believed Pauline's mother was trying to sabotage their relationship, so they went to unthinkable lengths to make sure that didn't happen.

Pauline and Juliet were polar opposites. Pauline was from a working-class family who lived in Christchurch, New Zealand. Juliet was from a well-to-do family in the U.K., and her father was a much-respected physicist. The pair crossed paths when Juliet's family moved to Christchurch, and the two teens found themselves in the same PE class.

However, both girls had suffered from health issues that rendered them unable to partake in the exercise class, and so sat together on the sidelines. While they sat out the class, they got chatting, and found they had similar likes and dislikes. From their appearances, the two girls were vastly different; Pauline was short, had dark hair, and a more introverted demeanor. Juliet, however, was tall and vibrant, her accent considered "posh."

Quickly, the girls began spending all of their free time together. The 15-year-olds had similar imaginations, and when they spent hours upon hours together, they'd create fantasy worlds and imaginary religions. One such fantasy realm became their obsessive form of escapism, and they named it "the Fourth World."

In addition to discussing this alternate world, the girls would write extensively about their fantasy realm, crafting pages upon pages of material centered around their land of make-believe. The girls wrote books and plays and intended to use this material to move to California with one another and work in the movie business.

The intense friendship raised concerns from the Parker and Hulme families. While they were happy their respective daughters had met a close companion, they began to think there was something more to the friendship. It was the 1950s, and homosexuality was still seen as a mental illness in New Zealand.

Still, despite their reservations, the Hulme family readily accepted Pauline into their home and even took her on their family vacations with them. Certainly, if they didn't, Juliet would become so sick with anxiety that she'd spend the entire holiday ill. She'd become so withdrawn without Pauline there that it served the Hulme family best if they didn't interfere in the teenagers' relationship.

As the friendship grew, so did their time in the imaginary world they'd created.

In 1954, when Pauline was 16 and Juliet was just on the cusp of turning 16, Juliet's parents announced their separation. In the midst of the divorce, the Hulme's were planning on sending their daughter to South Africa to live with other family members. Plus, it would do the young girl some good. She'd been so consumed, borderline obsessed, with Pauline that some time apart for the teens was seen as a good idea.

However, when the girls found out about the plans, they were heartbroken. The idea of being separated made them feel physical pain.

Juliet's parents had always been the more easygoing of the pair's caregivers. So, it didn't take long for the girls to convince them to allow Pauline to move to South Africa with Juliet. However, Pauline's mother, Honorah Rieper, would prove to be the obstacle in their way. She wouldn't allow her daughter to move to another country, thus scuppering the girls' lifelong plans of being together forever.

So, she had to die.

The girls would sit and mull over how best to do it. Pauline would write about it extensively in her diary, pondering *why, out of all the people who die every day, couldn't her mother simply die*? And while she was at it, she wished her father dead, too.

As teens, we've all done and said things we wince at now. From telling our parents we hate them or telling them they weren't good enough, we can all think back to awful things we've said out of teenage rage. This wasn't one of those things: Pauline truly wanted her parents gone so she could live her life with Juliet.

In the end, the girls concocted a finalized plan: to bash Honorah Rieper to death with a brick and make it look accidental. In her diary, Pauline underlined the day as "The Day Of The Happy Event."

On June 22, 1954, Honorah took her daughter and Juliet out for afternoon tea. The trio enjoyed a warm afternoon beverage before taking a leisurely stroll in the nearby Victoria Park, where the girls would carry out their nefarious plan.

Pointing to a pink charm they'd left on the ground as a way to distract Honorah, they began beating her over the head as she kneeled down to inspect the jewelry. The brick they used was encased inside a stocking. The girls took turns, swapping the bloodied weapon between them as they both battered the mother to death.

Once Honorah, blood pooling from her head, was dead, the girls hid the weapon in the woods. Then, as per the plan, they feigned horror and trauma as they raced back to the tea kiosk, screaming that there'd been a gruesome accident: Pauline's mother had fallen badly and banged her head. Both girls had blood spatters all over them.

It didn't take a seasoned detective to see this wasn't the scene of an accident. It was a murder scene. When investigators made their way to the park, it was clear as day that whoever had done this was full of rage. Honorah had been hit 20 times with a blunt object; even some serial killers don't end their victims' lives with as much brutality. The murder weapon was found crudely discarded not far from the scene.

Pauline Parker and Juliet Hulme were swiftly arrested. Unsurprisingly, the case garnered a lot of attention across New Zealand. For two young, seemingly polite and promising young girls to carry out such a barbaric attack was unheard of. The trial would become a spectacle, largely in part due to how sensational the prosecution's claims were. Well, they were sensational for the 50s: they suggested that Pauline and Juliet were in a relationship.

Whether they were romantically involved or not does not entirely matter: both girls denied these claims anyway. Being in a same-sex female relationship wasn't illegal (it was if you were a gay man), but the teens would still have been ostracized if it was discovered the relationship was romantic. Plus, intense teenage relationships can often border on obsessional, making the line between platonic and romantic very fine.

Still, the public bought into the sensational trial, which read out excerpts of Pauline's diary. In it, she would talk about the murder in the days leading up to it. She noted she was nervous but excited at the idea of getting rid of her mother. She mentions how the plan was to initially use a brick inside a sandbag as a weapon and spoke of her feelings of being "keyed up" as "The Day Of The Happy Event" got closer.

The defense centered around a folie à deux: the madness of two. They argued the girls had a shared mental illness, in this case, delusional disorder, and weren't of sound mind when they slaughtered Pauline's mother.

The trial came to a head in August 1954 when both Pauline and Juliet were found guilty of murder. Since they were under 18, their sentencing was much more lenient than had they been classed as adults when they committed it. So, they were given five years of detention, though the court made sure that they were sent to different prisons.

Their time in jail saw the teenagers grow up living out their worst nightmare: to be separate from one another and nowhere close to the life they'd dreamed they'd share together.

Upon their release in 1959, they were now young women. Despite their intense and passionate relationship during their teen years, it seems neither woman felt that much affection for the other anymore, and they never spoke again. Or, perhaps, they kept away from one another as they didn't want to be reminded of the horrific act they'd carried out together. It may even be that they were forbidden from speaking to one another again.

Or, like in a lot of youthful relationships, they'd simply grown up.

Now, even at 21, perhaps they still didn't see just how terrible a thing they did with one another. Regardless, neither of them would run into any trouble with the law again. Pauline was given a new identity and moved to the U.K., where she taught horse riding. Here, aside from working, she would become somewhat reclusive, her actions gradually catching up with her. It took years after the murder for Pauline to realize what she'd done, and according to her sister, she had been living in regret ever since.

Juliet lived a rather quiet life, too, until 1994, when journalists were able to track her down. By this point, she'd changed her name to Anne Perry. Anne just so happens to be living out Juliet's childhood dream of being a successful writer.

Anne's books were mostly murder mysteries, and over the years, she garnered many awards for her writing. She even wrote an instructional DVD on how to write called "Put Your Heart On The Page: An Introduction To Writing."

Naturally, the press requested comments from her as to how she felt about what she did as a teenager. She was adamant she didn't dwell too much on that since it would just be a way for her to torment herself.

She passed away at age 84 in 2023.

As far as we know, Pauline is still alive.

Hide And Seek

Floridian Sarah Boone said the death of her boyfriend was an accident, a silly game gone wrong. She claimed they were playing hide and seek when a terrible mishap caused Jorge Torres Jr's tragic death. She didn't bank on video evidence exposing this to be lies.

This case has yet to come to fruition, so there's not a great deal of content to offer, but I felt compelled to include it in this volume. The case has all the hallmarks of a true crime story that will present many gray areas before it's over.

In 2020, Sarah Boone, then 42, and her boyfriend Jorge Torres, were drinking together one evening in their Winter Park home when the pair agreed it would be fun if they put him inside a suitcase and zipped it up. Alcohol can make you do strange things, and when you're bored, drinking games can often turn bizarre, as it did in this instance. However, it would go from bizarre to macabre incredibly fast.

Once Jorge was inside the suitcase, Sarah left him inside the tightly zipped luggage to die. As he was gasping for breaths, she was recording it on her phone, taunting him all the while.

Slowly, Jorge suffocated to death.

It wouldn't be until the following afternoon that Sarah would call the police. Her version of events served to shrug off culpability. She said she and Jorge were drinking, and zipping him in the suitcase was something they both agreed to as a bit of fun. Sarah was adamant she left a small gap in the zipper so Jorge could make his way out. However, since they were drinking heavily, Sarah said she passed out and didn't wake up until the following morning. By this point, it was too late. Jorge hadn't gotten out of the suitcase and had suffocated to death. By the time she reached him, her boyfriend was beyond help.

She said she'd found him deceased that morning but admitted that it took until the afternoon for her to report it to the police. Her story was strange, to say the least.

When the authorities arrived on the scene, Jorge had injuries to his face and a bust lip. Again, things weren't adding up. Investigators immediately looked to Sarah as the prime suspect, not believing the death was accidental.

Still, she wasn't immediately arrested, though she was asked to attend a voluntary interview at the station the next day. Sarah did as she was asked and handed her phone over when the police asked for it.

Officers looked at Sarah's phone as she waited in the interview room. What they found would cause her story to crumble into a pile of ashes. She'd recorded Jorge in the suitcase as he pleaded, "Sarah, I can't breathe," while she said that this was for "everything you've done to me." At some points, she laughed, and he repeated her name again and again. "That's my name; don't wear it out," she replied.

When Jorge insisted that he couldn't breathe, Sarah said, "That's what you do when you choke me." At one point, her speech is clearly slurred, and she alludes to Jorge cheating on her.

After viewing the footage, officers quickly arrested Sarah on suspicion of murder.

However, the case isn't as open and shut as you may think. Sarah is expected to use the battered woman defense at her trial sometime in 2024, and her claims of domestic abuse can be propped up by prior incidents of abuse from Jorge toward her.

Prior to his horrific death, Jorge had been arrested numerous times for alleged bouts of domestic abuse against Sarah. Four of those arrests saw Sarah bail her boyfriend out of jail, and the pair resumed their relationship afterward. On one occasion, Sarah was the one arrested for strangling Jorge, though nothing came of this charge. The relationship was tumultuous, to say the least.

There is no outcome of this case as of writing, but the battered woman defense is something I'm highly interested in. I've written an article on the topic called *Battered Woman Syndrome and True Crime* (it's online if you're interested in learning more—that's the title word for word). I won't cover this subject here, but the article does pinpoint that a woman with Battered Woman Syndrome has three tragic outcomes:

1. The sufferer kills her abuser.
2. The abuser kills the victim.
3. The victim ends their own life.

Is this a case of number one? Or senseless, cold-blooded murder?

Vengeful Obsession

Young mother-to-be Alisha Bromfield was six months pregnant when her boss, 36-year-old Brian Cooper, brutally murdered her on August 18, 2012. The man was obsessed with the 21-year-old, and when she rebuffed his advances, he lashed out in the worst way imaginable.

Alisha was just one semester away from graduating with a degree in forensic psychology and criminal justice from Western Illinois University. Getting pregnant, especially before she graduated, had never been part of the plan. Add to the fact that the baby's father was choosing not to be in the child's life, and things hadn't panned out as expected for Alisha.

Still, with her baby girl just months away from arriving and graduation just around the corner, there was light at the end of the tunnel. Plus, her job at a garden center was offering her an attractive maternity package for when the baby was born. It would give Alisha time to bond with her baby and think of her next steps while juggling motherhood. She wanted to make use of her degree eventually, but for now, working at the garden center in northern Illinois felt like her best bet.

It funded all the things her little one would need upon her arrival. Plus, Alisha had fun with her co-workers, and clocking into her job gave her a chance to socialize and catch up with them. There was always one grouch at work, though: her boss, Brian Cooper.

It's an often-used stereotype that the older boss always berates and nitpicks his younger colleagues. However, in this case, the meanspirited boss seemed to single out one person in particular: Alisha.

Despite him being often cruel to the young employee, kind-hearted Alisha had been known to do personal favors for Cooper, such as walking his dog. It seems there may have also been another reason Alisha was so fearful of standing up for herself: she didn't want to be fired. She was so close to giving birth and needed that paid time off when the baby arrived.

It seems Cooper hung this over her head. He'd been overheard calling Alisha derogatory names, ordering her about, and even berating her in front of customers. Still, leaving wasn't an option. On occasion, Cooper was even known to throw things at Alisha when she didn't carry out the job to his liking. Or, it seems, when he felt the urge to act inappropriately hostile toward her.

The cruel boss threatened to cut her hours to keep her compliant. She had let him know just how much she needed the job, and as malignant people tend to do, he used this to gain an upper hand, chipping away at her weakness. Since she was pregnant, she would need to attend doctor's appointments every so often, but Cooper purposely scheduled her to work on these days despite having prior notice of her need to be off.

Amid his mistreatment of Alisha, Cooper would make it clear he was interested in her romantically. Even though she feared losing her job, she remained adamant that the pair were just friends. Cooper would persist and persist, however, which may explain his frequent angry outbursts at Alisha. He was getting more and more frustrated that she wouldn't go out with him. As can be the case with ego-driven individuals, rejection simply isn't an option for them. No does not mean no to them.

It's been reported that Alisha brought her complaints about Cooper to higher management, but her concerns weren't heeded.

Still, in August 2012, Cooper had an upcoming wedding to attend, and he wanted Alisha to be his plus one. With mere months to go until her little girl was born, the young woman felt she had no choice but to agree, lest she risk getting fired for whatever infraction Cooper would accuse her of. Once the baby was here, she'd finally be free. Until then, she was going to do her best to keep Cooper on her side. As always, she insisted she would only accept the invite as his friend.

When Alisha told her mother, Sherry, about the wedding trip, which would mean traveling to and staying in Wisconsin with Cooper, she was understandably worried. She'd heard all about her daughter's boss and his maltreatment of her. Still, Alisha did her best to put Sherry's mind at rest. She told her mother she'd made it clear she wasn't his date for the wedding and that she and Cooper were staying at the same hotel as all the other wedding guests.

The idea of there being safety in numbers worked somewhat in putting Sherry's worries to one side.

Alisha and Cooper drove to the Sand Bay Resort in Door County, Wisconsin, on August 17, though it wouldn't take long for an argument to ensue. When Alisha stepped foot in the resort, she was confronted with the truth: the wedding party wasn't staying at the same resort as them. It would just be her and Cooper. Alisha was upset she'd been lied to and texted her mother to tell her. She also said she was coming back home, which was a four-hour drive away.

However, a short while later, Sherry received another text from her daughter telling her that she'd decided to stay the night but was coming back first thing.

Cooper took Alisha's agreement that she'd stay as a green light to make more unwanted passes at her. Away from the confinement of the garden center, Cooper was free to act even more brazenly and inappropriately than usual. That's just what he did. So, Alisha told him she'd attend the wedding, but that was all; they'd go straight back home in the morning.

He'd broken her down to the point she was willing to accept him firing her.

The pair attended the wedding, though Cooper's behavior only worsened. The more he drank, the more inappropriate he became. Obviously, Alisha didn't touch a drop of alcohol, so endured his treatment of her for the entire night in complete sobriety. Her patience was wearing thin. By the time they got back to their hotel room—which had two beds—Alisha said she wanted nothing more to do with Cooper, and as soon as they got back to Illinois the following day, the friendship was done.

Cooper became incensed. He jumped on Alisha as she lay on her bed and attacked her. She begged him to stop, pleading with Cooper to remember she was pregnant. He didn't care. He violently pulled her from the bed and strangled her to death on the floor. In doing so, he also killed her unborn baby, who she'd already decided would be named Ava.

Hours later, Cooper made his way into a nearby gas station. He asked to use the phone, dialed 911, and turned himself in. "I'm a good person besides what I did last night," he told the operator.

Only, he hadn't told the operator everything he'd done that night. He didn't just brutally kill a promising young woman over her rejection of him; he defiled her corpse, too.

When the police arrived to arrest Cooper, he didn't resist and willingly got cuffed. Investigators then made their way to the hotel room Alisha and Cooper shared. Her lifeless body was on the floor, half covered in a blanket. Her naked body had blatant cuts and bruises, suggesting she put up a fight before Cooper drained her life from her.

When officers asked Cooper how he knew Alisha, he suggested they were dating. According to him, he wanted the relationship to develop more but had been respectful of crossing that line since she was six months pregnant. Ironically, this didn't seem to matter when he was strangling her to death.

He then told officers he got upset when Alisha told him there wasn't going to be a friendship once they got back home, and he saw red. After she went to sleep, he stayed awake, pacing the hotel halls and chain smoking. One idea he had was to tie Alisha up with his computer cord. He returned to the hotel room and woke Alisha from her slumber. He asked her to go on a cinema date with him the following day, which she declined.

He saw red again. He dragged her to the floor and strangled her to death. Once she was dead, Cooper decided he wanted to know what his victim looked like naked. He removed her clothing and sexually assaulted her corpse.

Brian Cooper was subsequently charged with two counts of first-degree murder as well as third-degree sexual assault of a corpse.

The more investigators looked into Cooper, the more apparent how obsessed he was with Alisha, frighteningly so.

He'd taped a mini camera in the bathroom trash can at their shared hotel room, which would have given him direct access to watch her as she used the bathroom.

You'd think Cooper would have no choice but to plead guilty, considering all of the evidence stacked against him. Not only that, he admitted to the murder in police interviews and even gave investors graphic details of how he assaulted her corpse afterward. But Cooper pleaded not guilty due to intoxication. His defense centered around the idea that he was too drunk to have any intent to murder.

This meant a trial ensued, causing Alisha's family to endure lengthy recountings of her murder.

Surprisingly, when the jury went to deliberate, they couldn't come to a definite conclusion. A hung jury was announced. It began to feel as if Cooper was going to get away with his crimes. If he didn't get away with them entirely, it certainly looked like he was going to get the lightest punishment going.

The next trial took a year to come to fruition, but when it did, Cooper was eventually found guilty of murder and sexual assault. He was given two life terms behind bars.

Alisha's mother, Sherry, had to endure not just one but two trials. Each one went over her daughter's death with a fine tooth comb, meaning the grief-stricken mother had to relive her child's murder multiple times. Each trial bolstered the feeling that she could have done something to save Alisha from her fate.

Deciding to channel her pent-up grief and rage into something productive, not self-destructive, she founded The Purple Project. The name came from Alisha's family banding together to wear purple, her favorite color, at her funeral.

The organization offers financial and emotional support to young single mothers, just like Alisha, who had felt forced to stay in a toxic job to support her and her child. The project also provides grief counseling and retreats for parents mourning the loss of a child due to murder.

In an unexpected twist, Sherry forged a relationship with Cooper's sister, Kellie. While she was initially nervous to do so, Kellie felt she had to reach out to Sherry and speak with her. The killer's sister had felt uneasy that her brother never truly took responsibility for his actions, and it weighed heavily on her that Cooper had ended a young woman's life so senselessly.

Meanwhile, Cooper has tried appealing his sentence to no avail. He remains behind bars.

Killer Shame

Filicide—the act of a parent killing their child—often occurs when the child is eight years old or over if the perpetrator is a male. When the child is young, statistically, it's more likely for a woman to do harm to the child.

The reason for filicide differs from case to case; sometimes it's a revenge killing, sometimes it's so the parent can get rid of their parental responsibilities, and sometimes it's because the killer was experiencing an episode of psychosis.

In this case, in the murder of 13-year-old Dylan Redwine, his father murdered him over some shameful pictures. Dylan had uncovered some intimate images of his father in compromising positions. When Dylan confronted his dad over these pictures, instead of listening to his son's concerns, he murdered him.

The images would have caused some embarrassment to the father; in one, he was depicted eating feces from a diaper. In another, he was wearing lingerie. For teenage Dylan, processing these images of his dad proved to be a struggle. Naturally, children don't need to be made aware of certain aspects of their caregivers' lives. However, Mark Redwine, fueled by shame, decided to kill his son instead of talking through his discovery of the private photos.

Redwine was divorced from Dylan's mother, with whom he had another son, Corey. Toward the end of 2012, Redwine was embroiled in a bitter custody battle with his ex, wanting full custody of their teenage boys.

In November of that year, Dylan visited his father, although he didn't want to. Unbeknown to Redwine, his son had seen his stash of pirate pictures and felt uncomfortable around his dad. Still, he would be forced to go since his mother was afraid of being prosecuted if Redwine didn't see his sons.

Dylan would never make it home to his mom.

Little is known about Mark Allen Redwine prior to his infamy after his bizarre reaction to feeling embarrassed over some explicit pictures. We know he was divorced twice and adamant his kids should live with him in La Plata County, Southwest Colorado. The area of La Plata County Redwine lived in was mountainous, perfect for embarking on treks or outdoor adventures up the plentiful rocky hills.

You'd think most 13-year-olds, perhaps boys especially, would love the rugged area and couldn't wait to visit. It was ideal for bike riding, exploring on quad bikes, or swimming in the plentiful nearby lakes. For Dylan, though, the thought of being at his dad's home in the mountains filled him with dread. He told his mother as much and begged her not to make him go on that cold November Sunday.

However, the mother of two felt fearful that Redwine would set his legal team on her if she didn't make Dylan go on the trip. Her attorney had warned her that while they were hashing out their custody agreement, the Redwine boys still had to see their dad.

Dylan didn't tell his mother why he didn't want to go; he just dreaded going. His older brother, Corey, knew why he didn't want to go, though. He'd seen the pictures, too. The brothers had kept it between them, unsure of what to do after finding the sexualized images on their dad's computer.

In one image, Redwine is dressed in women's underwear; in another, he has what looks like excrement on his face while holding a diaper. The teenagers took photos of the images on the computer before shutting it down. Then, they discussed what they'd just seen, sometimes laughing about it and other times confused about it. They agreed not to mention it to their dad right then and there, but it didn't take long for Corey to use it against his dad in an argument.

The father and son were having a heated quarrel over the teenager leaving empty bottles of alcohol around the house. Redwine texted his son images of the strewn bottles, to which Corey replied: *I have some pictures, too*, before sending Redwine the images of himself.

Dylan had confided in his mother's divorce and custody attorney about the images he'd seen on his dad's computer. He stressed to her that he wanted to live with his mom, though the attorney was powerless to do anything until the hearing.

On November 18, 2012, Redwine collected Dylan from the Durango-La Plata County Airport. There barely a word said between the father and son, and certainly no affectionate embraces or playful interactions between them. It was purely transactional. Dylan's lack of desire to be around his dad was seen when he tried to go see his friend who lived nearby, but Redwine put the brakes on those plans. He demanded his son stay in the house with him.

Still, Dylan texted his friend, and they made plans to meet up early the following morning, just after 6 a.m. When Dylan didn't show up the next day, his friend texted him. There would be no reply.

Redwine reported his son missing that day. The father stated he'd left his property early that morning and, upon his return, discovered Dylan was gone. A search of the nearby wooded areas ensued, followed by a larger-scale search of the vast mountainous area. While the search party was out until late at night, Redwine was in his home. It was easy to get lost in the desolate area, particularly in the dark, so it was unusual he chose to turn all the lights off in his house when Dylan was out there somewhere, potentially lost and alone. The lights could have offered him a guide to safety.

Not everyone believed Dylan had simply taken off, though. Certainly not his mother or his brother.

As part of the investigation, officers spoke with many people, some of them just to get a better idea of what Redwine was like as a person. Though there was no evidence to tie him to his son's vanishing, they still had to cover all bases. His ex-wife—the one before he married Dylan's mother—asserted he said some chilling things while they were married. One of them was that if he ever needed to dispose of a corpse, he'd do it in the mountains. When they were getting divorced, he spat at her that he'd kill their children before letting her have them.

Redwine's son from his first marriage, Brandon, learned of his half-brother's disappearance and got in touch with Corey. Brandon had somewhat lost touch with his father of late, but he was keen to help find his sibling. He traveled to his father's home to help with the search party, of which Redwine wasn't a big part. It became clear to Brandon that his father had no real interest in searching for his son.

Corey, Brandon, and Redwine's brother, David, all had to sit him down and try to get him to be more actively trying to find Dylan. "Get involved," Brandon pleaded with his father.

It seemed like, the next day, Redwine had heeded the group's pleas. Along with Brandon and David, they drove up the mountainous roads, hoping they could get even a glimmer of a clue. After less than half an hour, Redwine wanted to turn back. "He's not up here," he announced when they went up Middle Mountain Road. It was then Brandon figured his dad knew something everybody else didn't.

He even asked his dad if he knew where Dylan was. *Yes*, Redwine replied. "He's in my heart."

The search for Dylan persisted, though notably without much help from Redwine, despite the fact he knew the area better than anyone. Over seven months passed before human remains were found on Middle Mountain Road. They were Dylan's.

Brandon noticed his father was unusually unaffected by the discovery. He called Redwine "stoic" throughout the whole ordeal. Once Dylan was confirmed dead, Brandon had an odd interaction with his father. Redwine was saying how they'd not be able to tell if the cause of death was blunt force trauma unless they had the skull. Brandon felt like his dad had given himself away and unintentionally confessed to how he killed his son.

Still, there wasn't enough evidence to secure an arrest. In 2013, in a bid to clear his name of the suspicion surrounding him, Redwine went on a talk show to give his version of events. Dylan's mother was also on the show, and the parents would end up arguing. One interesting aspect of the appearance was that the show's host offered Redwine the opportunity to take a lie detector test to see if he really didn't have any ideas about how Dylan died.

Redwine declined the polygraph test.

The suspicions surrounding Redwine weren't just from friends and family; the police were also keeping an eye on him. In August 2013, they sent cadaver dogs to see what they could sniff out in Redwine's home. The clever dogs detected the scent of human remains in the washing machine and in the living area. They also let the dogs sniff the clothing Redwine was wearing the night he picked Dylan up from the airport.

They detected the scent of human remains.

The following year, the dogs were used to pick up any possible scents in Redwine's truck. Yet again, the dogs alerted the handlers to the scent of death.

However, there was nothing to charge Redwine with. Everything was circumstantial; highly incriminating but still just circumstantial.

Then, at the beginning of November 2015, Dylan's skull was found on Middle Mountain Road. The area was so vast that the multiple search teams missed it. An animal attack was ruled out as the cause of death.

Years after Dylan's death, his father, Mark Redwine, was arrested and charged with murder and child abuse. How Dylan died was another question altogether. A forensic expert at the trial said Dylan had a fracture just above his left eye and more marks on his skull that were indicative of a knife. These injuries were determined to have been caused at (or around) his estimated time of death.

It was put to the jury that Dylan's confronting his father over the explicit photographs caused him to fly into a rage and attack his son fatally.

On October 8, 2021, Redwine was handed 48 years in prison for killing his son. The tragic case has an odd irony for Redwine. He killed his son out of shame over the images he'd seen. By lashing out and murdering him, the images were then posted online, causing thousands of people to access and view them.

He still denies murdering Dylan.

Snatched From The Womb

On April 24, 2019, Marlen Ochoa-Lopez's husband contacted Chicago PD to report his wife missing. It was especially urgent since she was nine months pregnant, ready to give birth any day now. It wasn't like her to simply take off, particularly at such an important time. Even so, the police couldn't do anything until 72 hours had passed.

Meanwhile, nearby, Clarissa Figueroa was also making her own call to 911. She'd just given birth at home, but the baby wasn't breathing. The dispatcher sent an ambulance to Figueroa's home immediately, and she and the baby were rushed to the hospital. The baby was stabilized and taken to intensive care.

Still, the doctors and nurses were used to seeing new mothers and newborns. Some things just didn't make sense about Figueroa and her baby. Notably, the woman didn't have blood on her lower half, as you'd expect. She had it on her torso and face, though. An internal exam also showed it was unlikely the woman had just given birth. The nurses were beyond suspicious, though they didn't raise their concerns with family services for a fortnight.

The presumed father of the child, Piotr Bobak, quickly set up a crowdfunding page for his child's funeral. The baby hadn't died, but he claimed it was highly unlikely the little boy would survive.

As Figueroa and her partner raised money and posted about their newborn on social media, Marlen Ochoa-Lopez's family was desperately looking for her. Her due date had come and gone. If she'd taken off somewhere, which was highly unlikely, she'd taken none of the baby's items. She had no money, no resources, and no connections. The family knew something bad had happened.

On May 7, 2019, there was finally a clue: the police were alerted to social media posts on a group for mothers-to-be. Marlen had got talking to Figueroa, who offered her some baby items. Marlen agreed and, on April 24, made her way to Figueroa's home to pick them up. She'd never been seen again.

The police headed to the Figueroa household, but the woman wasn't home. Her young daughter was, though, and she directed the police to the hospital where her mother was laid up. Here, they would question the woman about her knowledge of Marlen's last known movements. Figueroa admitted she knew of Marlen but denied she'd been with her the day she vanished. Investigators didn't believe her, particularly since the mother-to-be's car was found parked up near Figueroa's property.

All signs pointed toward the woman's involvement in the disappearance. The police looked into her past, including her recent social media posts.

It was uncovered the new mother had previously had her tubes tied, making getting pregnant highly unlikely. About 1 in 200 women who receive this treatment wind up getting pregnant afterward; that's 0.5%. Still, apparently, she'd just delivered a baby boy. Figueroa passed it off to family as a "miracle."

When the police spoke to the woman's neighbors, it was found that being pregnant didn't quell the mother's desire to smoke and drink. She'd been doing both while she'd been "pregnant." Still, she joined an online group for expectant mothers, and a search of her post history revealed she'd taken an explicit interest in mothers who were giving birth around May time. This group was how she met Marlen.

There was one thing investigators could do to tie Figueroa to Marlen's disappearance. It was a sensitive topic, but this was a troubling case that needed solving: DNA test the baby and see if Figueroa was, in fact, the biological mother.

She wasn't.

Figueroa was no longer a person of interest. Investigators were sure they had a killer in their midst. They obtained a warrant to search her home, and unsurprisingly, it was filled with incriminating evidence. Tragically, Marlen's blood covered various parts of the home. The worst discovery was yet to come.

Marlen's mutilated body was stuffed inside a trash can. Her torso had been sliced open to remove the baby, her neck blue from the cable that was wrapped around it.

There was no denying what had happened, but there was another shocking twist to come: Figueroa's daughter, Desiree, admitted to helping her mother kill and dispose of Marlen.

Desiree said Marlen was lured to the home under the guise of free baby clothes. Once the 19-year-old arrived, the mother and daughter made her feel relaxed, chatting with her on the sofa. Once distracted, Figueroa crept up behind Marlen and strangled her to death with an electrical cable. Then, once the victim was no longer breathing, they cut the unborn child from his mother using a kitchen knife.

The pair then got rid of the body by crudely shoving her inside a trash can before calling 911 over the "birth" of the baby boy.

Sadly, due to oxygen deprivation, the little boy only survived just over a month.

Figueroa and Desiree were charged with murder. Desiree complied with investigators and agreed to testify against her mother. In the end, Desiree got 30 years in jail while her mother got 50 for the sickening murder. Figueroa's boyfriend, Piotr Bobak, got four years for his part in cleaning up the murder.

Safe With Me

This case is more recent, and due to the young age of the victim, not a great deal has been published about the crime.

In 2023, Scotsman Andrew Miller, who previously went by the name Amy George, abducted a primary school pupil while dressed as a woman. He lured the girl into his car by offering the younger a ride home. She agreed—but was taken to the accused home and sexually abused for more than 24 hours.

Former butcher Miller, 53, is said to have previously identified as transgender but has since expressed the desire to be referred to as male. Some news outlets have reported that Miller was in the process of transitioning sex, but throughout his trial, he was referred to as "he" and has been detained in a male prison since his arrest. Miller has expressed his desire to be referred to as "he" moving forward.

Normally, this wouldn't have been something I would mention—sexual assault is just that, no matter the perpetrator's gender. The reason that this was mentioned in court is that Miller allegedly used his presentation as a woman to lure the child into the car. The court cast doubt that the girl would have entered the vehicle if she knew the driver was biologically male.

Miller was described as "wicked and predatory," and his crime had "clearly involved a substantial component of planning."

Once the sexual deviant got the 11-year-old into his property, he carried out prolonged sexual abuse on the girl. Again, details are sparse on this, but it's been made clear throughout his trial that his offenses toward the child were heinous. He also made her watch pornography. He forced the youngster to sleep in the same bed as him, and once he fell asleep, she managed to sneak to his landline phone and call the police.

Officers arrived at Miller's home within minutes. Police entered the property and discovered the suspect in their underwear with one silicone breast in and tights on.

The victim was taken to safety, although there's no doubt it'll take some time before she can overcome the horrors that Andrew Miller forced her to endure.

When the police spoke to the little girl, she said she got in Miller's car because she thought it was a woman offering her a lift. She described the woman as seeming kind and wanting to help her. This ruse soon dropped when Miller got his victim back to his home.

A further search of the man's property found almost 250 indecent images of children.

In police custody, the attacker denied abusing the girl, insisting that he picked her up because it was cold and it was a motherly thing to do. Upon getting the girl confined at his house, she asked to leave a number of times, but the abductor refused. He told the terrified girl that she was his "new family."

While being questioned, Miller seemed more concerned about how his arrest would adversely affect the transgender community rather than the wellbeing of his victim.

In early 2024, he was handed 20 years in prison for this abhorrent crime. No doubt it'll take more than that for his victim to come to terms with her 27 hours of hell with her attacker.

Since then, Miller has made an appeal to have his sentence reduced. He feels his gender identity was too heavily scrutinized and didn't play a part in his offending. His defense advocate said that Miller suffers psychological difficulties, and his prior non-offending should be taken into consideration.

His appeal was rejected.

Brutal Rage

This case is horrifically gruesome. So much so that when looking at the crime scene pictures, I shuddered. The sight of blood doesn't usually affect me this way; I can look at evidence and grizzly photos and use them to understand the facts of the crime.

Not in a cold, inhuman way—I'm still affected by these horrific images—but I think I have a pretty strong stomach for those kinds of things.

In this story, though, I had to take a break from my desk to process the vileness and the violence of the crime and the agonizing murder of Maria Nemeth. She was killed by her boyfriend, Fidel Lopez, in 2015. Let me warn you again: this case is exceptionally brutal. The killer pulled his girlfriend's insides out with his bare hands.

I first read about this crime a few years back, and even reading about it made me wince. But when I was compiling the evidence and crime scene photos for this volume, I was utterly repulsed by Lopez's actions.

Maria Nemeth was a 31-year-old free spirit who—as cruel fate would have it—crossed paths with Fidel Lopez, a fiery 25-year-old. She wouldn't know the hot temper her soon-to-be love interest would have—how could she? He was charming and caring, at least in the beginning.

The pair first met in a club in Florida, and their relationship developed quickly. Maria had just emerged from an eight-year marriage, and Lopez's situation was far more complicated: He was juggling fatherhood while living with his child's mother.

Still, Maria persisted with the partnership. It's unknown if he'd shown episodes of violence towards the young woman prior to his fatal—and barbaric—attack on her. The brutality of the crime may suggest that this wasn't Lopez's first instance of showing his violent side.

Their relationship deepened. Maria and Lopez moved in together, eventually settling in the picturesque area of Sunrise, Florida. Shortly after, though, the unthinkable would happen: Maria's life would end barbarically at the hands of her partner.

Maria had taken on the role of the complex manager of their new home. Things seemed to be going in the right direction for the young couple. A steady job and a boyfriend of almost a year by her side saw Maria happy and content.

Then came that horrific night. On September 20, 2015, the pair were drinking in their brand-new apartment, celebrating their new abode. Clinking shots of tequila before downing them, basking in the joy of how good life was getting.

The couple began a drunken dance around their new home, eventually finding themselves in the bedroom closet. Here, they got intimate. This is where things took a sinister turn for Lopez. He carried out acts of violence so barbaric it's stomach-churning to think about.

As the pair got intimate, Lopez said she used her ex's name twice. It's important to note here that Maria had been with her ex for almost a decade. Considering she'd had a few drinks, you can understand this indiscretion. Of course, this would have hurt Lopez, but if he'd taken the time to think about her mishap, he would have realized it wasn't the huge sin he thought it was.

But, drunk and full of anger about Maria's mistake, Lopez became incensed. He began stomping around their new apartment, breaking things, punching the walls, and completely shattering their sliding doors. He was upset, there's no doubt about it, but his violence wouldn't stop at making holes in the walls—he soon turned his violent attention to Maria. The woman was lying in the closet, having drifted off from the copious amounts of tequila the pair had consumed.

It was at this point Lopez began carrying out the unthinkable. He used a beer bottle to violently violate his partner in her vagina as well as her anus. When this didn't satisfy his brutal urges, he found her hair straighteners and used those to continue his violation of his victim.

Then, the crazed man began using his hands on his partner's insides. He pulled her insides out, leaving them strewn next to her limp body. As you can imagine, Maria was bleeding extremely heavily by this point after so much monstrous violence had been directed toward her intimate areas.

The man took some time to regather his thoughts, going outside for a cigarette. It slowly dawned on him what he'd done: the finality of the acts he'd just carried out. He returned to the lifeless woman and lifted her up. He carried her to the bathroom and held her head above the sink, cupping handfuls of water before splashing it on her face manically. She didn't wake up.

Lopez was in a state of panic now. He quickly began trying to clean up the bloody mess from the senseless attack he'd carried out on Maria before calling 911.

His clean-up left a lot to be desired—there was still bloody tissue on the floor when police arrived. Initially, authorities suspected Maria had killed herself from a botched abortion she'd tried to carry out. How they thought a woman could—or would—rip her own intestines out is beyond me.

A further inspection of the property saw officers notice not only a large amount of blood on the floor but also the destruction throughout the apartment. An officer also noticed chunks of bloody tissue on the floor, specifically inside the closet. The trail of blood—and the amount of blood—was a disturbing sight, even for seasoned detectives.

The emergency responders checked for any signs of life on the woman, but their attempts to revive her were futile. Maria was pronounced dead in the early hours.

The police spoke to neighbors who told them they heard a man's voice in the adjacent apartment, screaming and shouting. They also said they heard loud bangs and other bothersome noises that lasted for about 2 hours. Lopez was cuffed, bundled in a police car, and immediately taken to the station.

In the investigation room, Lopez told a tall tale: he insisted that Maria had wanted him to insert the objects—and his entire arm—in her. It was how they got intimate, he said.

Afterward, he claimed Maria went into the bathroom because she felt unwell and perhaps needed to throw up. No doubt she felt ill after such "consensual" brutality.

Lopez then claimed he walked in on her a few minutes later, checking in on her to make sure she was okay. It was at this point he noticed Maria was struggling to breathe.

As you can imagine, the police didn't believe Lopez. They urged him to tell the truth.

It took a while, but he did eventually. "She called me the name of the other guy," he complained. *Not once*, Lopez stressed, but Maria called him the wrong name *twice*.

Was Maria's unintentional mistake hurtful? It must have been. But the reaction she got for it was simply unhinged, uncalled for, and barbaric. Lopez could have walked away, cooled off, and spoken to her when they were both sober. Instead, he took her life in one of the most brutal ways I've ever heard.

Lopez was then charged with murder in the first degree as well as sexual battery. There was no way he could claim innocence after his confession and the abundance of evidence against him. He pleaded guilty to these charges, taking the possibility of the death penalty off the table. Instead, he was handed life behind bars.

In one fit of rage, Fidel Lopez took a young woman's life away. He stripped a loving family of their beloved daughter and sister. He also ruined his own life—and for what? An accidental mishap. A slip of the tongue.

I feel a great sense of sorrow when I think of Maria's family. I just don't know how you'd get over a loved one dying in such a torturous manner. The only hope I have is that she was unconscious throughout it and felt nothing of the brutal things Lopez did to her.

What Happened To The McStays?

The McStay clan was the picture of perfection. Husband and wife Joseph and Summer, along with their young sons, Gianni and Joseph, made up the loving family. They lived in the affluent area of Fallbrook, California, and had a life many people can only dream of.

Joseph, 40, owned his own business, and Summer, 43, was a real estate agent. Gianni and Joseph, four and three, respectively, adored their parents and were the life and soul of the family.

The day started as any other on February 4, 2010. Joseph headed out to work, and Summer carried out household chores. Joseph had called his dad, Patrick, at some point through the day but had to end the call prematurely due to being late for a meeting. However, the day wouldn't end as normal, which would have seen the parents serving up dinner before putting on a movie for a night on the sofa.

February 4 was the last time anyone would hear from the McStays.

It took a few days for the family to grow concerned. By February 13, Joseph's brother grew so unsettled by his brother's sudden vanishing that he broke into the McStay's home. The whole family had been trying to reach Joseph for well over a week, and it wasn't like him not to keep in touch. He spoke to his father almost every day. So, Michael McStay entered the property via a window to see if there were any clues as to where his brother and his family had gone.

The family dogs were there, but they had run out of food and water, though thankfully, they were still alive. For animal lovers like me who always wonder what happens to abandoned pets in situations like this, I'll let you know: the dogs survived and were looked after by friends and family. The older dog went to Summer's mother, and a friend of the couple took in the McStays' new puppy.

Michael was naturally alarmed. A further look around the property showed food had been taken out of the fridge and just left on the kitchen counter; it was like they'd left in a hurry.

The police were called, and an investigation into the disappearance of the McStays was opened. Detectives were surprised to find that the house was in order; there was no blood found on the property, and nothing had been stolen. It didn't look like a crime scene at all. It looked like the family had left of their own free will.

As such, it was impossible for detectives to get access to the couple's bank statements. There was no evidence to suggest the family were victims of a crime, so they had no grounds to look at their financial records. All law enforcement had to go off in terms of clues were the couple's phone records and the grainy footage of the McStay's neighbors' CCTV.

Detectives retraced the family's last known movements. They confirmed that Joseph's business partner, Charles Merritt, was the last person to see him.

Merritt also admitted to talking to Joseph twice that day when he was driving home. According to Merritt, Joseph was possibly stopping off to grab some food before heading home. Investigators then started looking for Joseph's car, which they soon discovered had been towed from an area close to the Mexican border.

It seemed as if the case may have been solved: the family had headed for a fresh start in Mexico. This theory was further propped up by some CCTV showing a family—a man, woman, and two little boys—making their way into Mexico City the same day the McStays had vanished. Then, a more in-depth look at Summer's search history seemed to suggest that she'd been making plans for a new life across the border and seeking out Spanish lessons.

Joseph's mother was handed the footage to see if she could confirm if the man in the footage was her son. It was grainy CCTV, but even then, the mother knew that it wasn't her son. She'd know his walk a mile off, and whoever was in that video, it certainly wasn't Joseph.

Still, there were numerous reported sightings of the family, though these leads always turned up nothing. For a short period, another of Joseph's business partners and an ex-boyfriend of Summer's were on the police's radar, but they were eventually cleared of any involvement in the disappearance.

Two months after the family was reported missing, the FBI got involved. Still, every lead took them to a dead end.

It would take another three years before there'd be a break in the case. A biker driving off-road in the desert found human remains in Victorville, California, about an hour and 45 minute drive from the McStay family home. When the police were called, the case got even more macabre: there were two graves, each with one adult and one child. The bodies had decomposed terribly in the desert, but the forensic team was still able to use the teeth of the corpses to gain positive identification.

The bodies were Joseph, Summer, Gianni, and Joseph Jr. They'd been killed by blunt force trauma.

What had been a missing persons case for over three years was now a murder case with the violent culprit still at large. A new look at Joseph's vehicle, which had been towed away three years prior, found some new DNA. It was quickly tested and came back with a positive match: it belonged to Joseph's business partner, Charles Merritt.

However, Merritt passed a lie detector test years ago when they interviewed him. He seemed concerned and upset over the family's disappearance.

Now, though, they looked back on his old interview transcripts and realized that Merritt had been talking about his business partner in the past tense the whole time. At the time, the McStays were simply missing. Merritt was talking as if they were already dead.

Because he knew they were already dead: he'd killed them.

A deeper look into Joseph and Merritt's relationship showed it had been strained. Merritt owed Joseph tens of thousands of dollars, which he always made excuses not to pay. For a long time, Joseph let this go, knowing Merritt had a gambling problem.

It seems Joseph was no longer willing to be lenient and demanded his money.

More detective work revealed that Merritt had forged checks in Joseph's name just after the family vanished. When they traced his cell phone around the time of the McStays murder, it pinged as being in the same desert where the family were buried.

It was suggested that the search queries on Summer's computer about a new life in Mexico were all carried out by Merritt after the murder to make it look like the family had started life anew across the border.

Then, there was the confusion over Joseph's car being parked in a random area near the border. It was theorized that Merritt drove it there and abandoned it to help prop up the idea that the family was in Mexico.

Towards the end of 2014, over four years since the family was brutally killed, Charles Merritt was arrested for their murders. It took a further five years for his trial to start, and in 2019, he was found guilty of each murder. He was sentenced to death.

In 2022, a documentary was released that covered the McStay case and questioned whether Merritt was truly guilty. The program offered a comprehensive look at the evidence and even an interview with Merritt himself. Many viewers felt as though there was enough reasonable doubt to acquit Merritt. Others think he's as guilty as the court found him.

He remains on death row.

Final Thoughts

Thank you for reading *Unbelievable Crimes Volume Eleven: Macabre Yet Unknown True Crime Stories.*

In a change of pace from other installments, this volume includes 20 cases. Moving forward, each volume will have more cases than the typical 10 or 11, which feels like the right move for this anthology. Hopefully, you prefer this format. It also means there's a higher chance there are a few cases you've never happened upon before.

In this installment, I've covered some truly wicked crimes. All of them are abhorrent and thought-provoking for differing reasons: the case of Kim Wall is utterly sickening due to the sheer brutality she suffered. She wasn't just killed—she was mutilated before she met her untimely end. The fact that we'll never know what truly happened before she was murdered is haunting. In all likelihood, our brains probably can't even conjure up the evil she was exposed to before her life was ended.

The case of Pauline Parker and Juliet Hulme shines a morbid spotlight on children who kill. We often find it hard to comprehend children as cold-blooded or innately corrupt, and in a rare twist, this case doesn't ask us to. There's no doubt these teen girls committed an atrocious, irreversible act, though it wasn't carried out because of hatred or bloodlust. When you think of that, you think of Mary Bell or Sharon Carr, two girls who killed out of sheer enjoyment. The young culprits in this case were immature, naive girls who'd been wrapped up in cotton wool their whole lives. They were certainly old enough to know what they did was immoral and heinous but too immature to understand the implications of it.

Sexual assaults and sexually motivated crimes are, without a doubt, tough to learn about. Sometimes, the details of these cases are enough to make you set the book aside and gather your thoughts. To put yourself in the victim's shoes—as true crime followers invariably do—is draining. To feel some small semblance as to what the victim felt in those moments, the fear, the dread, the terror, is heartbreaking. Following feelings of deep empathy for the victim are often feelings of deep rage toward the perpetrator.

This brings me back to the question I posed in the introduction: *is true justice ever possible when a life has been taken?*

Hopefully, this volume has introduced you to crimes you've never heard of. I know the term "unknown crimes" is subjective, but I do try to ensure the cases I cover aren't widely known, even in the true crime community.

Once again, I'd like to thank you for reading. As always, I truly value your readership. Crime can be a tough topic to dive into, and I know it can make us second-guess how much we think we know people. (This reminds me of my dad's favorite quote that I've not recited in a while: *Always expect the unexpected.* I've actually toyed with the idea of starting a new series with that as the title, covering cases where the perpetrator was someone extremely close to the victim who *almost* got away with their crimes. Let me know what you think!)

If you find the time to leave a review, that would be so helpful in getting the book to a wider audience, and I'd be extremely grateful. I truly hope you enjoyed this eleventh installment of the series. If so, book twelve is due out soon!

I hope to see you there and, until next time, take care.

Daniela

My newsletter sign-up link:

Danielaairlie.carrd.co[1]

---

1. http://danielaairlie.carrd.co

Don't miss out!

Visit the website below and you can sign up to receive emails whenever Daniela Airlie publishes a new book. There's no charge and no obligation.

https://books2read.com/r/B-A-GFMW-ESIKD

BOOKS 2 READ

Connecting independent readers to independent writers.

Also by Daniela Airlie

Infamous Crimes
Infamous Cults: The Life and Crimes of Cult Leaders and
Their Followers

Unbelievable Crimes
Unbelievable Crimes Volume One: Macabre Yet Unknown
True Crime Stories
Unbelievable Crimes Volume Two: Macabre Yet Unknown
True Crime Stories
Unbelievable Crimes Volume Three: Macabre Yet Unknown
True Crime Stories
Unbelievable Crimes Volume Four: Macabre Yet Unknown
True Crime Stories
Unbelievable Crimes Volume Five: Macabre Yet Unknown
True Crime Stories
Unbelievable Crimes Volume Six: Macabre Yet Unknown
True Crime Stories
Unbelievable Crimes Volume Seven
Unbelievable Crimes Volume Eight

Printed in Great Britain
by Amazon